THE
NONPROFIT
FUNDRAISING
SOLUTION

Powerful Revenue Strategies to Take You to the Next Level

Laurence A. Pagnoni,
with Michael Solomon

AMACOM

AMERICAN MANAGEMENT ASSOCIATION

New York • Atlanta • Brussels • Chicago • Mexico City • San Francisco
Shanghai • Tokyo • Toronto • Washington, DC

Bulk discounts available. For details visit:
www.amacombooks.org/go/specialsales
Or contact special sales:
Phone: 800-250-5308
E-mail: specialsls@amanet.org
View all the AMACOM titles at: www.amacombooks.org
American Management Association: www.amanet.org

This publication is designed to provide accurate and authoritative information in regard to the subject matter covered. It is sold with the understanding that the publisher is not engaged in rendering legal, accounting, or other professional service. If legal advice or other expert assistance is required, the services of a competent professional person should be sought.

Library of Congress Cataloging-in-Publication Data

Pagnoni, Laurence A.
 The nonprofit fundraising solution : powerful revenue strategies to take you to the next level / Laurence A. Pagnoni, with Michael Solomon.
     pages cm
 Includes bibliographical references and index.
 ISBN-13: 978-0-8144-3296-9
 ISBN-10: 0-8144-3296-4
 1. Fundraising. 2. Nonprofit organizations—Management. I. Title.
 HV41.2.P34 2014
 658.15'224--dc23
                                                            2013020756

About AMA

American Management Association (www.amanet.org) is a world leader in talent development, advancing the skills of individuals to drive business success. Our mission is to support the goals of individuals and organizations through a complete range of products and services, including classroom and virtual seminars, webcasts, webinars, podcasts, conferences, corporate and government solutions, business books, and research. AMA's approach to improving performance combines experiential learning—learning through doing—with opportunities for ongoing professional growth at every step of one's career journey.

Printing number

10 9 8 7 6 5 4 3 2 1

This book is dedicated to my dear sister, Lorraine McDermott (1945-2011), who taught me my ABCs and who watched over me in life as she does now in heaven. I dedicate this book to her not just because of her passing, but because she always believed in me with unflinching devotion. That belief made me a better person and a better fundraiser for the nonprofits that I love.

CONTENTS

ACKNOWLEDGMENTS

IN WRITING, I HAVE BEEN blessed with fine colleagues and collaborators, whose beautiful talents have made this book all the better. Enormous thanks to Sheldon Bart, an author in his own right, who first said to me, "You have enough articles, write a book!" and who helped me do just that all the way long. Thank you Ben Goldman, a nonprofit CEO who walks the walk. Ben's review of my drafts and feedback has been invaluable. My esteemed gratitude goes out to Sean Jones, Sara Kirkwood, and Bob Serow for their technical help along the way, and to Steven Lapkoff, who transcribed our interviews and chased down leads with poise and alacrity.

Bob Nirkind, my editor par excellence, gently and resolutely shepherded me through the publishing process. I am truly grateful for his gracious partnership. His patience and insights have enriched me, and this text, to no end. Julia Lord, my wonderful agent, both pointed the way for me and held my hand as I embarked, for which I am deeply indebted to her.

Michael Solomon, my muse and conversationalist, expertly worked with me to maintain a human voice throughout the book. Moreover, he made it fun! His probing questions and relentless appetite for clarity, precision, and stories drawn from my own life led to a more accessible manuscript, a fulfilling collaboration, and a lasting friendship between us.

Special thanks to my partner, Wei Ng, who patiently listened to all my ups and downs, and our sons, Carlos and Jose, who help me remember why I write in the first place. Thank you team!

Finally, I am indebted to the nonprofit leaders, trustees, volunteers, and funders with whom I have had the privilege of working, many of whom have been my clients. Thank you for showing me how to serve. To paraphrase one of my Jesuit teachers, our true joy is to know that our life has been of service.

Laurence Pagnoni
October 2013

If you would like to ask the author a question or leave your comments about the book, please go to www.thenonprofitfundraisingsolution.com. Forms, checklists, and grids that correspond to the book can be found there, and you can also sign up for Laurence's free weekly e-newsletter.

THE
NONPROFIT
FUNDRAISING
SOLUTION

Introduction

I **NEVER SET OUT TO** be a fundraiser; I became one of necessity. I began my career as an executive director, working for nonprofit organizations in Virginia, California, and eventually New York City. During my time as an executive director, I managed every facet of the organizations I led, including all aspects of their fundraising. I soon came to realize how essential adequate revenues were to ensuring a nonprofit mission. Without them, our visions for a better civil society amount to little more than pie in the sky.

Mark Twain once advised people to be careful about reading health books because "you might die of a misprint." I'm a big fan of Twain's poignant humor, and so when writing this book about nonprofit fundraising, I tried to keep his advice in mind and convey vital information carefully. I can assure you that nothing you'll read in this book will kill you or your organization. Chances are, though, that you are already experiencing something like stagnation, which, for those of us who have dedicated ourselves to "changing the world" through nonprofit work, can sometimes feel like its own sort of death. You dream, you sacrifice, you persist, and yet all too often you come up against a brick wall in trying to achieve real success for your mission. The issue isn't that you lack the requisite desire or dedication to excel. The problem is you lack the money to implement your vision. It's a lament that is so common in the nonprofit sector that I sometimes think I hear it in my sleep.

Subsequent to my time as an executive director, I've served non-profit clients as a fundraising counsel for more than eighteen years in my capacity as chairman of LAPA Fundraising, an organization I founded in 1995 in New York City. I've had the privilege of offering or participating in countless conferences, seminars, workshops, and panel discussions aimed at helping nonprofit organizations raise more money. What I've noticed is that although the venues and the audiences change, the questions people ask rarely do. Whether we're in a house of worship, a university, or a conference center, in front of big audiences or tiny conclaves, someone inevitably steps forward and asks: *How can I get to the next level?* That is, how can my nonprofit raise more money and create the conditions for sustainable success and high impact?

"Good question," I usually say, although a more accurate response might be, "Good and *very popular* question." The issue of how to get a nonprofit to the next level is nearly ubiquitous because most nonprofits in the United States are small or midsize organizations, and some 87 percent of them are trying to change the world on annual revenues of less than $1 million. Fully 73 percent exist on less than $250,000 per annum. Many of these organizations ended their last fiscal year with deficits.[1] These numbers aren't just sobering; they indicate quite clearly that unless these trends are somehow reversed, the future effectiveness of nonprofits in America looks gloomy indeed.

Fortunately there *are* a number of tried-and-true ways to get you to the next level you seek. The book you are about to read is my attempt to show you how to do so, and to help you answer that seminal question for yourselves, your donors, your constituents, your boards of directors, your communities, and most importantly, your clients. I like to say that a nonprofit is making progress when each day it gets to confront a better set of problems than it had the day before, or, in this case, better questions. My hope is that once you've implemented the ideas and tactics I've outlined, you'll never again need to ask, "How do we get to the next level?"

We all know your nonprofit requires funding to operate. A limited ability to secure revenue means a meager chance to fulfill your mission. But your success at fundraising is more complex than a simple discussion of dollars and cents because it communicates a profound message about your organization's health and well-being.

Through your fundraising program, you inform members of the community about your moral imperative and your impact on their lives, and you inspire donors to work on your behalf. Most of all, your fundraising program reflects the effectiveness of your overall organization. It's a litmus test of your viability.

The central premise of *The Nonprofit Fundraising Solution* is that organizational development and successful fundraising are inextricably linked. Married, if you will. Your organization will do better by seeing itself as a multifaceted entity with fundraising entrenched firmly at its center. Why? Because the barriers to better fundraising performance are, so often, the same obstacles to organizational growth. The task for your nonprofit on its way to the next level is to approach fundraising with as much passion as you have for ameliorating the social problem to which you've dedicated your mission. Getting to the next level has as much to do with organizational development as it does with the fundamentals of fundraising. These two elements need to work in lockstep. The tendency in the past has been to treat fundraising as if it existed in a vacuum, separate and distinct from the other parts of your organization.

A 2013 report released by San Francisco–based CompasPoint found:

> *[H]alf the chief fundraisers … expected to leave their current jobs within two years due to an assortment of pressures, including a frequent feeling that they're out on a limb because they're expected to produce results without having enough backup from bosses and boards that haven't managed to put effective, systematic fundraising plans and approaches into place.*[2]

Too often, fundraising programs exist in a silo. The fundraiser works in isolation, and the fundraising program is not integrated into the day-to-day activities of the organization. This is a pervasive and grievous condition.

A large number of the individuals asking how they can get to the next level come from nonprofits that might be described as *high-performing*, *underrecognized*, and *underresourced*. In some cases, their agency has relied on one dominant funding source for too many years. In others, their private foundation grants program is rudimentary or largely inactive. Their individual donor program, if they even have one, may also be weak, while they usually have no planned giving program whatsoever. In all probability, their organization has no staff members focused entirely on fundraising, and their board of directors isn't working efficiently as a team and maximizing its strengths, nor is it very knowledgeable about its role in fundraising.

Make no mistake, I'm not trying to be Jim Collins, author of *Good to Great*, although I am trying to pick up where he leaves off. Many nonprofit leaders buy and refer to works by Collins and authors like him, yet they are baffled as to how to apply these theories to their real-world dilemmas. They want to use Collins's research, they know it's the right stuff, but they lack the revenue to implement the theory. They don't know how to raise *all* the money needed to, in Collins's words, go from good to great. They have figured out how to raise enough money to remain in existence, but they lack the tools to get to the much-desired-but-just-out-of-reach next level.

The revenue program of the typical nonprofit needs more love and care than most executives admit because without a robust revenue engine, the best ideas or strategies wither on the vine. This book aims to fill the important gap between theory and the practical methods used to secure that needed revenue—down-to-earth, detailed steps that can be implemented immediately.

HOW TO USE THIS BOOK

Fundraising is a practitioner's craft. It requires the intuition of the artist and inquisitiveness of the scientist. It needs flexibility to pilot new approaches and time to gauge their effectiveness. It's neither primarily theory (although good theory is required), nor wishful thinking or magic. It's not a matter of manipulating your address book. Fundraising is grounded in hard reality, and central to the task is building thoughtful relationships with prospective donors who are value aligned, meaning they care about what you do and do not want to live in a world where what you do is absent.

There is no one-size-fits-all method of organizational development or fundraising, either. Every nonprofit organization has a unique mission and strategy for supporting that mission.

The Nonprofit Fundraising Solution is divided into two parts. The four chapters in Part One, "What Getting to the Next Level Really Means," articulate my theories about some of the key aspects of organizational development and explain how to focus on getting your organization ready to execute a robust fundraising program. The ideas that they contain lay the mental groundwork for what advanced fundraising requires. Written from the perspective of the fundraiser, Part One looks at how the issues of organizational culture, leadership, board governance, and higher-level thinking are fundamentally tied to fundraising.

In Part Two, "Advanced Fundraising Tactics to Raise Revenue," the tactical aspects of fundraising that I've utilized and refined the most are addressed. These chapters cover the nuts and bolts of advanced fundraising. Each of the nine chapters addresses a particular fundraising tactic that you can use. Some of the topics may be familiar to your own fundraising activities, but my take on them may provide a new perspective. Depending on your organization's unique personality, you can modify all of these tactics to accommodate your particular needs. It may require considerable work on your part, but it's also what will bring you greater revenue.

At the end of many chapters you'll find a Casebook, in which I use a real-life story to illustrate the subject at hand. "At the End of the Day," which is the designation used to close each chapter, emphasizes that chapter's main points as you move to the next one. All the organizations and cases referred to in this book are real, though most names have been changed.

The development of relationships is central to fundraising, be it a relationship to a group of donors, to the community, corporations, service providers, your peer nonprofits, or the world at large through social media. These kinds of relationships build the profile of your organization. The tactics used to foster relationships create confidence in your agency; they attract financial support and, most importantly, they enable your nonprofit to deliver its mission as effectively as possible.

I strongly urge you to read Part One as a whole before you turn to Part Two. To get to the next fundraising level, it will take more than a few clever "modifications" to set you on the right course. The correlation between fundraising performance and organizational development is too often overlooked, yet that's precisely what getting to the next level is all about. Your organization and your way of thinking about it inevitably have to change. You may have to become better at documenting the impact of your programs. You may have to generate better client or program outcomes. Your leadership or your board may need some redirection. Or you may have to alter your culture to become more amenable to the fundraising process.

The chapters in Part Two are designed as stand-alone topics and can be read in whatever order you choose. They are chock-full of real stories that come out of my fundraising experience. Some may make you laugh, others might cause you to cry, but hopefully all contain nuggets of road-tested knowledge to help you on the way to truly achieving your mission.

My own expertise as a fundraiser is in addressing these issues from the perspective of someone who understands how money propels mission into action and has a real impact on the quality of life of the individuals and communities that nonprofit organizations serve. Once you understand the issues of organizational culture, leadership, board governance, and higher-level thinking, and see how they are related to fundraising success, implementing the tactics in Part Two will come naturally.

There is never one moment when we arrive at being the best fundraisers we can be. It's an ever-evolving and unfolding process where continuous education and reflection on our experiences are required. Having lived them myself, I understand the stresses and challenges you face in building capacity and growing your organization, and I have the experience to help guide you toward that goal. I've worked with my clients to build effective revenue engines within their nonprofits, and I want to do the same for you in this book.

WHAT I WON'T BE COVERING AND WHY

Finally, a mention about what won't be covered: fee-for-service income by nonprofits. At first blush, the idea of a nonprofit earning income might seem like an oxymoron, but *earned income* (fees paid to a nonprofit for services rendered to you and me, plus governmental fees, or the money a nonprofit charges government for delivering services) accounts for 73.5 percent of total nonprofit revenue for U.S. charities.[3] The estimated percentage of fee-generated income varies somewhat according to how one classifies different revenue sources. This book only addresses *contributed income*; that is, income donated by individuals, foundations, corporations, and other potential givers. I made that choice because I'm not an expert on earned income and many good books have already covered the subject. A colleague once said to me, "I hate when I go to conferences where they talk about nonprofit fundraising and act like the 26.5 percent that's contributed income is the entire picture." His words are especially prescient given the new models of social venture hybrids. Earned income is now the primary revenue engine of the U.S. nonprofit sector and numerous international growth models. I don't deny it. I just want my readers to know there are greater authorities on that subject than me.

I think we can all agree that one of the most wonderful aspects of nonprofit work is how much potential it has to truly change the lives of others in a meaningful way. Through the work of nonprofits, enormous social problems, as well as smaller, more personal ones, can be rectified, mitigated, and eliminated as society itself is advanced as a whole. I know you've come to this book with most of the key ingredients to make that happen, like a stalwart ship on a great ocean of possibility. All that remains is to summon some powerful, long-lasting wind for your sails.

PART ONE

WHAT GETTING TO THE NEXT LEVEL REALLY MEANS

CHAPTER ONE

WHY ORGANIZATIONAL CULTURE IS CRITICAL

YOUR NONPROFIT PROBABLY SEEKS TO realize a vision for a better society—everything from ending the AIDS epidemic, to building permanent housing for the homeless, to preserving Native American culture. There are a multitude of missions, yet each is inextricably bound to one simple truth; namely, that adequate revenue is essential to accomplish it. In fact, an organization's ability to raise revenue and to spend it effectively is among the most important signs of its sustainability.

There's a line in an old German play called *Schlageter* that goes, "Whenever I hear the word 'culture' ... I remove the safety from my Browning [pistol]!" While I trust you don't hold such extreme views about the topic at hand, you may be wondering why a book about nonprofits begins with a chapter on culture, of all things. As you'll see, the culture of a nonprofit, though not always conspicuous, is nevertheless the principal driver of every organization's ability to advance. And that organizational culture, taken together with its fundraising implications, is a key indicator of how well that organization will ultimately be able to fulfill its mission.

In this chapter, we'll examine:

• How we define organizational culture

- The three critical aspects of a nonprofit's organizational culture: whether it is dependent on a dominant source of revenue or multiple revenue streams, the extent to which it is inwardly or outwardly focused, and the capacity of an organization to revisit its fundamental assumptions
- What it takes to change organizational culture in order to achieve the next level of mission impact

Despite the primacy of needing sufficient revenue, most nonprofits in the United States have organizational budgets of less than $250,000 and are never able to grow past this threshold. They are stagnant. No matter how you look at it, there is a striking disconnect between their dream of a better world and the reality of that dream ever being fulfilled. That, in my humble view, is a true call to arms.

HOW DO WE DEFINE ORGANIZATIONAL CULTURE?

I happen to be writing during an economic downturn—really, a downturn one week, an uptick the next, and a flat line the following week. Nevertheless, it's a period of declining or flat endowments and major donor giving, meaning that revenue shortfalls are acutely preventing organizations from achieving their visions. Nearly every nonprofit I know of is strapped for cash, and many have shelved growth plans. Yet, in spite of these prevailing circumstances, I can still cite hundreds of nonprofits, from tiny organizations to massive ones, that defy this characterization and have met, if not exceeded, their revenue goals. How did they accomplish this?

We know for certain that even at peak phases of the business cycle, the nonprofit sector is grossly undercapitalized.[1] One reason (among many) is that certain hidden dynamics prevent an organization from raising more revenue, and thereby stunt its growth and thwart its vision. Peter Drucker, the "father of modern management," dubbed it the informal reality of an organization (as opposed to the formal definition of its structure). Drucker discovered that this informal reality is the true driver of an organization and how it is run. For example, some organizations are highly entrepreneurial. In the nonprofit world, entrepreneurial organizations are often those that are predominantly outcome-oriented. They emphasize quality assurance and outcome measurements and focus on customer service. Other organizations are heavily bureaucratic. They emphasize leadership hierarchy and compliance with a rigid schedule of reports and procedures. An executive I met who had gone to work for an international children's charity not long ago remarked, "This place is more corporate than IBM, where I used to work." The level of bureaucratic requirements at the children's charity was something he never expected to find in the nonprofit world. In other words, he experienced "culture shock."

So what exactly is organizational culture? Business textbooks define it as those "values and behaviors that contribute to the unique social and psychological environment of an organization." This definition isn't necessarily wrong; it just misses the way an organization's culture operates in reality, and how those values and norms engender habits that either lead to or preclude success. While it's true that history and shared values form culture, in my experience, the most important element shaping an organization's culture is leadership.

Consciously or not, the mentality of an organization's leadership permeates every office and cubicle of the nonprofit. The leadership of a nonprofit steers the priorities of the organization, including its fundraising strategy. But organizational culture doesn't just end there. Every member of the organization—the CEO, the board of directors, and the professional and administrative staff—contributes to the culture, and therefore should understand how it operates so as to build an element of organizational vitality rather than, as is too often the case, a blunt instrument of indoctrination. A bludgeon, if you will, of poorly crafted conformity.

THREE CRITICAL ASPECTS OF A NONPROFIT'S ORGANIZATIONAL CULTURE

From a fundraiser's point of view, there are three critical aspects in a nonprofit's organizational culture. They have to do with the choices made concerning the dominant source of revenue versus multiple revenue streams, the extent to which an organization is inwardly or outwardly focused, and the capacity of an organization to revisit its fundamental assumptions.

A Dominant Source of Revenue vs. Multiple Revenue Streams

The nonprofit sector has distinct revenue streams that exert a powerful influence on each organization's culture. Organizations typically become wedded to a single dominant revenue source and, to some degree, it shapes the board's and staff's perceptions of reality. A nonprofit that subsists on government contracts will likely develop a strong financial office to manage those contracts. And even though its board of directors may also be closely connected to private wealth, the organization never sees the possibility of exploiting those connections to cultivate individual donors. It is culturally blind to it because everyone's too stuck in thinking that "we get our funding from government." The individual giving program remains nonexistent or embryonic, at best.

Similarly, a sluggish nonprofit that barely survives on membership dues may be reluctant to solicit grants or major gifts because doing so seems alien or bothersome. The same revenue single-mindedness may be true of an agency funded primarily through hosting a gala event. Consider this call I received from a religious-based food pantry that wanted to add a grant program to its fundraising program.

"How have you been raising money to date?" I asked.

"Through one major annual gala and six smaller events throughout the year," the person answered. "It's been that way since we were founded fifteen years ago."

This food pantry depended on special events, so it concentrated on booking a celebrity for the annual dinner because 75 percent of its fundraising for the entire year comes from ticket sales to the gala event. "Why bother with other types of fundraising," their thinking went, "when you can get by just throwing a handful of parties every year?" This is precisely how a single revenue stream influences or, rather, overinfluences an organization. It's the proverbial tail wagging the dog.

Other organizations build full-throttle individual donor programs because they are dependent on a large number of donations to support their good work. But their "multiples" of revenue occur in the same way within the same revenue stream (which is not to be confused with true, effective diversification, which I'll discuss later in greater detail). They try in vain to construct a mountain out of $50 checks.

We often speak of culture as being ingrained or embedded. In each of the previously mentioned cases, we can detect a singular focus on one particular fundraising tactic that excludes, *ipso facto*, all other fundraising approaches. While these self-imposed restrictions are indicative of a lack of flexibility and a certain reluctance to depart from customary ways, what's worse is that they cripple the fundraising program by curtailing revenue and thereby limiting the success of the organization. That's why, when culturally deciphering your organization's revenue streams, you must grasp the degree to which rigid, inflexible thinking about fundraising may be blocking its path. This sort of self-awareness can then give rise to more positive, flexible thinking, which will correlate to higher revenues.

In some fundraising programs, flexibility may simply mean finding multiple rivulets within the same revenue stream. For instance, a nonprofit living off *federal* contracts may need to seek out opportunities for *state* funding, to minimize its vulnerability to congressional budget cuts. Or consider the nonprofit that relies on major gifts. It may be well advised to cultivate smaller gifts to fuel the next phase of major giving by cultivating more donors, some of whom may eventually contribute at higher levels. The point is to go deep within one revenue source, instead of going wide to many different sources or sticking (out of habit) with what's already not working.[2]

An Organization's Inward or Outward Focus

The second critical aspect of organizational culture, from a fundraising perspective, is the inward or outward focus of the nonprofit. What do I mean by these two distinctions? Typically an inwardly focused organization lives in a cocoon of its own making, managing its programs with little concern about the larger community that surrounds it, whereas an outwardly focused organization tends to mark its territory externally, through advertising, marketing, public relations, and other types of community outreach. Neither of these perspectives is faulty; in fact, many organizations will cycle through more inwardly or outwardly focused periods as their needs change. But too frequently we see extremes of inwardness or outwardness and, as the expression goes, therein lies the rub. What further complicates this conflict is that discovering which way a nonprofit leans, inwardly or outwardly, and to what degree, is usually easier for an outside observer than it is for members of the organization itself, so the problem is often not readily apparent to those it afflicts. Indeed, many organizations never reflect on this element of their makeup at all.

To better illustrate the perils of cultural imbalance, let's take a look at the Neighborhood Services League (NSL), an inward-focused nonprofit that was required to reformulate its approach to fundraising because 80 percent of its funding came from only one funder: city government. The NSL sponsors a number of human services programs such as housing, day support, and case management that are highly effective in helping a variety of people in need. NSL had expansion dreams, based on the real needs of its clients, which the current funder simply couldn't afford. When senior managers developed a five-year plan for future growth, they discovered that their projections fell millions of dollars short of what was required. Hence, they needed new funding partners and a new development approach; consequently, they elected to ratchet up their grant-seeking and establish an individual donor program.

Unfortunately, as effective as the NSL was in providing social services, it was for all intents and purposes invisible in the community at large. You'd even ask a few NSL clients whom they received their services from, and they'd answer, confusedly, "I think that's the city." While many, if not most, nonprofits suffer from poor branding, Neighborhood Services League, with its utterly nondescript name and otherwise anonymous presence, was distinctive in its wholesale lack of marketing distinction. "But we have our newsletter," the executive staff would say in defense. True, but bereft of a marketing plan, NSL never properly branded its name or expanded its network, and thus languished in obscurity.

An organization with an inwardly focused culture, like NSL, may do well with certain revenue streams (e.g., government and foundation support), but it shoots its fundraising program in the foot when it comes to soliciting individual donors or seeking grants. Even if the fundraiser uses state-of-the-art donor prospect researching techniques to identify potential donors, high emotional investment is required to secure high-level gifts. The willingness of individuals to give depends on how they feel about your organization. If prospective or current donors have never heard of your organization, no matter how much good it does, the emotional context for the donation doesn't exist and instead has to be manufactured, which takes considerable time and effort. Similarly, the grant-seeking idea was handicapped because, as any grant writer will tell you, when you apply for grants, funders want to know what collaborations you have with other nonprofits (and often they'll insist that you have them because they are a sign of your organization's credibility). The NSL was an island unto itself; it had no collaborations, nor did it have Memorandums of Understanding with any other agencies to procure services for NSL clients.

NSL's problems aren't unique; rather, they are the classic result of an organizational culture that is too inwardly focused. Before we examine how to dig NSL and others out of this rut, or avoid it altogether, let's take a look at what can go wrong with a cultural focus that looks too far outward. The best way to describe that type of organization is to think about Hans Christian Andersen's classic tale "The Emperor's New Clothes." The agency that is too outwardly focused, in its advertising, its promotional materials, and at its annual community ball, prances about, boasting about its effectiveness even as the social problems that it is supposedly tackling go … well, untackled. Its programs don't work or fall well short of the needs of its clients and the goals of its mission statement, yet the CEO is great at telling a (largely untrue) story about the agency to all who will listen. The United Way of the 1980s was a case in point. Its television ads were stellar, well produced, and ubiquitous, but many of its partnership efforts with its membership organizations left much to be desired.

If you discern that your organization is too inwardly or outwardly focused, here are some ideas for how to correct your issues.

Too Inwardly Focused
- Survey your funders or organize a listening tour. Even if they are government funders, ask them open-ended questions such as, "How do we compare to our peers?" or "What is your impression of our capacity and our ability to meet our client's needs?"
- If individual donors fund your organization, arrange to meet them and ask the same sort of open-ended questions.
- Report back to your board and process the feedback with them.
- Ask your funders, "Are there any other organizations with whom we should partner?" I once asked a nonprofit client's

main foundation funder this very question and he answered: "I've been waiting for your organization to ask that question for the last five years."

Too Outwardly Focused

- Do a listening tour of clients to see how the program is working for them. Truly listen. You could also survey your clients using either focus groups or online survey tools such as Survey Monkey. Once the results are obtained, share them with those who gave the input.
- Reexamine how much exposure the board and administrative staff have to the program. They may be too distant from the mission advocacy of the program and need to be brought closer through a regular volunteer experience or immersion tour.

It's instructive to consider how an outwardly focused organization creates the groundwork to ask for private money from individuals. The Salvation Army, one of the largest nonprofits in the world at this writing, is an excellent example. The "Army" wisely sets aside a significant budget for paid commercials during the holiday season. The cost of the TV commercials will be repaid by many years of sustained giving, because the image projected in those spots—the woman ringing the bell—has touched the hearts of millions. The bell rings from a rooftop where a family waits to be rescued in the midst of a flood, the bell rings in a dark alley where a homeless man sleeps. The commercial gives the viewer a visceral experience of the Salvation Army's mission in action. The values of the organization are clear, and the expression of those values invites a response from all who witness the spots.

The bell in these remarkable ads tolls for all of us in the nonprofit sector, too. It tells us that fundraising and marketing go hand in hand. The impact the nonprofit has on its community is the *product* the fundraiser is *selling* to the prospective donor. An inwardly focused organization needs to think strategically about developing the kinds of programs that will amplify its impact. But it first has to understand the way its culture limits its impact and, as a result, its capacity to connect with individual donors. Even if it chooses to stay inwardly focused, it should at least be conscious of that choice. Too many nonprofits never consider their options and never decide.

They just follow the traditional paths marked out by their organizational culture and usually wind up in the same place with the same dilemmas.

The Capacity of an Organization to Revisit Its Fundamental Assumptions

We began this chapter about culture with a reference to Browning pistols, so as we move toward the end, let's instead have a peaceful discussion of an organization I'll call the Peace and Justice Center. This nonprofit hosts weekend seminars on progressive issues in a rustic, idyllic setting. The Center has been around for a long time, but its adherents have aged (the average age is now 62) and attendance at its seminars has markedly slipped in recent years. It has lived off a single revenue source—seminar fees—for most of its history and has perennially been inwardly rather than outwardly focused. However, the Center has made some minor efforts to correct these faults. In recent years, it started a grants program. It has also been active in individual donor solicitation and is seeking to raise its organizational profile as well. But it's still a failing, stagnant nonprofit, struggling to meet its annual budget each year. One donor referred to it as "anachronistic." Back in the organization's heyday, from the late 1960s through the late 1970s, there was a greater focus in society on communal processes for peace and justice transformation. But moving into the 1980s, that tendency was eventually eclipsed by the personal growth, personal transformation movement. The Center never knew what to do with the shift or how it might adjust. The reasons illuminate the third critical aspect of organizational culture: the capacity of an organization to revisit its fundamental assumptions.

It is ingrained in the culture of some organizations to ask hard questions about their fundamental purpose and operations. Other organizations simply bury their heads in the sand. Not only does the Peace and Justice Center fall into the latter category by failing to detect the changing demographics and hence the concomitant needs of its donors, it misses the opportunity to reframe its fundraising strategy and rebrand itself for the future. The Center has traditionally seen itself as a provider of seminars. It considers each seminar as a separate, discrete entity and it is not used to thinking in other ways or being open to new ideas. If it only looked at its operations in a larger perspective, it might see that it could reframe its purpose and rebrand itself as a sponsor of peace-and-justice *projects*.

Suppose the Center designed a series of retreats with an overarching theme? Suppose the organization created an "Agenda for a Rational Tomorrow" that could be developed by a series of weekend seminars focusing on different aspects of the concept? If each individual seminar in the series was marketed as a facet of a larger effort, it might draw more participants, and if some of those seminars were led by personalities popular with youth, it might also draw younger participants. The whole package could be more compelling and attract more funders, and at the end of the series the Center could evolve into an attention-getting product. It might then conceivably realize its dream of playing a more vital role in national debates.

But the Center doggedly resists changes to its culture, and because of the way its culture has evolved over the past fifty years, it simply cannot entertain fundamental challenges to the way it does business. Hopefully that will change, but until it does, the Center will likely struggle on indefinitely with dwindling finances and the same insoluble dilemmas.

WHAT IT TAKES TO CHANGE ORGANIZATIONAL CULTURE

We said earlier that organizational culture is not always readily apparent, but oftentimes people within a nonprofit actually are aware of the problems caused by their culture. They don't employ terms like "organizational culture" around the watercooler, but they chat among themselves about what needs to be done to straighten out their agencies. Sometimes a planning process can be the appropriate corrective measure, but not necessarily. In fact, this "straightening out" doesn't ordinarily happen unless and until new leadership is put in place. The organizational leadership and any planning process that it undertakes to change culture are critically linked to one another, particularly in times of change. As they depend on each other for success, they therefore should not be separated.

All planning processes have to take place at the right time. One of my former clients, Supportive Housing Inc., put out a request for proposal (RFP) for a consultant's help in constructing a strategic plan. As any well-meaning consultant might do, I asked for a conversation with the CEO when I received the RFP.

"Nick, I have one question. How long do you intend to stay?" I asked.

There was an uneasy silence on the other end of the phone. Finally I said, "Um, Nick, that's not the answer I was hoping for."

In fact, this was precisely what I feared. A CEO usually can't lead or support a planning process and have one foot out the door. It's not fair to the agency when any plan the CEO comes up with ends up being inherited by someone else, because the parties involved in the process may feel duped later on. Planning processes work best with a leader who is either in it for the long haul or new enough to be curious about what will work best for the organization, instead of reacting to new ideas by explaining why they won't work. This is part of what makes the problem of changing a culture so intractable.

A planning process is likely to be most effective for cultural change under three circumstances:

1. A new CEO takes over or the current CEO intends to stay at least another three years.
2. Board members have a high level of curiosity about why they're having the same problems over and over again.
3. Enough resources, including financial, can and will be allocated to support the process.

You'd be surprised at how many planning processes are terribly underfunded. I heard of an acquisition—one nonprofit buying another—in which the acquiring nonprofit didn't have the $25,000 needed for rebranding, so the acquisition is still sitting there a year later, uninitiated. As with any initiative your agency undertakes, be sure to plan your funding and fundraising accordingly.

NEW STRATEGIES CAN MEAN NEW VITALITY FOR YOUR NONPROFIT

As a fundraiser with marketing training, I can appreciate how difficult it is to take a new product to market. When a new product is taken to market, it always arrives with an attendant batch of complexities and fears. In fundraising, we often ask nonprofit organizations to adopt a new approach, invite new people to the board, hire a new type of staff or outsourced contractor, or adopt a new fundraising strategy to use with a new group of donors. But we do so with a purpose, because new strategies often are highly lucrative and they can be implemented faster than most people think. So be conscious of your organizational culture and its assumptions. By moving toward a more open culture you will likely raise more money. Most important, new fundraising strategies can bring new vitality to the culture of a nonprofit, and greater success in fulfilling its mission.

Nonprofit CEOs, whether alone or in concert with a board member who is genuinely interested in fundraising, must set the tone and be the catalyst for a more assertive fundraising culture. This can in turn create fundraising leadership which emanates from every aspect of your organization; volunteers coming forward, a staff well-versed in the workings of your revenue engine(s), and trustees who ensure that fundraising strategy is in place, understood, appropriately funded, and eventually, reviewed for its performance.

The examples discussed in this chapter illustrate not only *why* organizational culture is critical for the success of nonprofits, but *how* it is critical for success or failure. The optimal culture requires laser focus, energy to implement, and a clearly articulated vision of where you're headed in the first place—the qualities of exemplary leadership. The next chapter discusses how the right leadership for a nonprofit creates the conditions for raising more revenue and therefore greater success in achieving an organization's mission. The passion and the vision of the gifted leader—one who creates a culture based on reflection, flexibility, and decisive action—guides the organization to the next level and to a better set of problems, which is the very definition of organizational growth.

———— ∾ **CASEBOOK** ∾ ————

The American Canyon Society (ACS) circulates scientific and historical information about the canyons of America, and has done so for the past forty-five years. ACS publishes a quarterly journal and also sponsors a series of symposia for scientists and outdoor enthusiasts. The journal was initially a black-and-white affair with little original content. In recent years, a new editor took over and turned it into a handsome, color magazine with new contributions from writers who donate their time. But the cost of the updated journal vastly exceeded budget.

The ACS was in a quandary about how to make ends meet. One of my colleagues, who sat on the ACS board of directors, presented a detailed development/fundraising plan for soliciting foundation and corporate support, as well as individual donations to finance a number of modest initiatives. He worked on the plan with the board's knowledge for more than three months. Some of the board members were intrigued. The president of the ACS, however, didn't want to engage in outside fundraising because he was afraid the organization would "become crass and lose its independence."

What dilemma did the ACS face? (Choose one.)
a.   It was living beyond its means.
b.   The new editor of the journal should have observed budgetary constraints.
c.   It should not have contemplated new initiatives until the journal was made solvent.
d.   None of the above.

If you answered "none of the above," then we're on the same page. The problem with this organization had nothing to do with the cost of its journal, but rather with the limited thinking of the president and others, which had become ingrained into the organization's culture. They could only see who they'd been for forty-five years, not who they were capable of becoming.

In the case of the ACS, the officers and board were accustomed to asking their members for dues; they did so reflexively (as they did whenever any financial crisis threatened) and uniformly, assuming that everyone had the same capacity to give. Membership dues were their sole source of revenue. When my colleague, a trustee trained in fundraising, proposed that ACS segment the membership dues according to each member's capacity to give, his new idea was dismissed as "too aggressive." Culture prevailed, in a mentality that can be summed up as: "This is how we've always done it before and will continue to do again." The obstacle was a cultural one, rather than just one person's stubborn view. It had literally progressed to the level of group-think.

Clearly, the ACS needed to look itself in the eye and tell itself the truth: Unless it stopped holding itself back from diversifying its revenue, it would never stabilize its finances, let alone advance to the next level of its mission. The unimaginative leadership of this organization mistook "principled" inaction for stability and preservation of the organization's identity. It sought to maintain the culture of the ACS, a culture of discord and stagnation, rather than convert it into a culture of success and fiscal responsibility.

Unsurprisingly, a change in leadership brought about a change in the ACS organizational culture as well. The new president, unafraid of fundraising innovation, sought out corporate sponsors, who took out ads in the ACS journal. He also solicited sponsors for an annual gala. Now the ACS has money in the bank and, as a result, is finally able to meet its debt obligations and publish its journal. Not only that, ACS successfully updated its website. The site is no longer a static Internet placeholder with information about how to join the ACS, but a full-fledged informational crossroads and bulletin board for the entire community of people interested in the canyon regions, with breaking news stories about research and new developments in the field. ACS is now on the way to becoming a well-capitalized organization, with dreams of an oral history project about the canyons of America and cash stipends for graduate students to attend international scientific conferences.

Similarly, the entire fundraising strategy has evolved from a reporting function to one of active stewardship. There is lively time and thought devoted to giving strategies, meeting new donors, and corporate underwriting. Board meeting agendas have shifted from the staid and simple reporting of "here's what we talked about" to action agendas with up-to-the-minute details about grants in the works and new sources of corporate sponsorship.

The fear of innovative fundraising that defined the ACS identity has been transformed, through culture, into the fulfillment of a larger and better mission.

AT THE END OF THE DAY

Ignore organizational culture at your own peril because you won't get depth in the fundraising program unless the culture is aligned with the fundraising goals.

CHAPTER TWO

LEADERSHIP FROM THE BELLY OUTWARD

MY FATHER WAS A STRONG Italian guy with even stronger opinions. He believed fervently in the value of solid leadership and eventually became an organizer with Teamsters Local 463. One of his favorite expressions was "the fish rots from the head back," which was his way of saying that poor leadership is almost always the root cause of an organization's failures.

I carried that maxim in my brain all the way from childhood through graduate school and my post-graduate management studies and, like most of my fellow management students, I eventually became a devotee in the cult of leadership. The mental picture of the fish was messy, but the metaphor seemed wise and enduring. But last year, on a whim, I decided to look up the expression "a fish rots from the head back." I was surprised to learn that several cultures have similar sayings, including the Greeks, the Turkish, and even the ancient Egyptians. But I was downright shocked to learn that those wise cultures, not to mention my father, were dead wrong about the dead fish. It turns out a fish rots from the belly first, not from the head.

That quickly got me wondering if my dad's pithy descriptive not only had its biology wrong, but perhaps its metaphor, too. Does "rot" really originate at the top of an organization? My own investigation leads me to believe that the fairest answer to that question is the Talmudic one: It depends. While I've come to believe that solid leadership is critical, so much emphasis has been placed on it as to improperly diminish the roles of following, challenging, and working *with* the leader. Not enough responsibility for success or failure is given to the "followers"—that is, to the staff, trustees, and professionals who make an organization's cause active in the world. I'm not saying good leadership doesn't matter; it's just vastly overrated. In my view, the art of following, or "followership," is the belly of your organization. Like it or not, organizational rot is title-neutral; it can set in among the workers just as easily as it can at the top.

So how do you, as a fundraising leader, not only prevent institutional demise, but also create the conditions to raise more revenue and thereby achieve greater success?

In this chapter, we'll examine:
- The importance of good followership
- The style of leadership that's right for your organization
- What a fundraising leader does
- The four most common roadblocks to successful fundraising
- Practical ways to apply the lessons of leadership to fundraising
- How to know if your leadership is working

Let's begin by examining leadership, though this time from the belly outward.

THE IMPORTANCE OF GOOD FOLLOWERSHIP

It's a pity that being a follower gets such a bad rap because everyone involved with fundraising ought to have the opportunity—even the responsibility—to act as both decisive leader and conscientious follower. The writings of the eminent Harvard leadership professor Barbara Kellerman have helped me to develop my own intuitions concerning the dynamic and mutual influence between leaders and followers. She defines followers in two ways: First, they are subordinates who have less power, influence, and authority than their superior. This is the more conventional view; the low men on the totem pole view, as it were.

Kellerman then breaks with prevailing wisdom by asserting that followers are definable not solely by their relatively low position in the hierarchical pecking order, but also by their behavior. In other words, whether they agree to go along with what someone else wants and intends, followers have the power and the ability to exert influence within an organization. A real-life version of the powerful follower was fourteen-year-old Malala Yousafzai, a "powerless" Pakistani teenager whose fight for educational rights against the Taliban became an international cause célèbre at the end of 2012. Either by critiquing the judgment and actions of their superiors, or by agreeing to affirm and implement the leaders' ideas and values, followers can play a decisive role in how leaders may act and what they can achieve.[1] In short, followers exercise power even in dissent.

I've seen confident leaders in the nonprofit world actively encourage their staff to wield the power of the organization, which has an even further, ancillary value of spreading the burden and helping the leader feel less lonely at the top. When judiciously applied, good leadership from the top fosters even more leadership among the collective. Effective followers can keenly monitor outcomes, question assumptions, formulate detailed proposals, keep colleagues honest and informed (including supervisors), initiate recommendations, and nurture and support coworkers and supervisors alike.

The most highly functional organizations—the ones that not only survive but flourish—tend to be led by individuals who are able to listen meaningfully to their constituents and thereby nurture their leadership traits. Even in my own company, LAPA Fundraising, good followership is a highly valued criterion in our hiring process—we actively seek people who are willing to speak out for the good of the organization and the clients we represent. True, we must still follow our client's leadership even though we are often at odds with it, but a good follower may (surprise!) even turn out to be a potential new leader and useful to our sector's future.

A lack of good followership is symptomatic of poor leadership, although in order to qualify as good, followership must still follow certain rules. It is likely proactive and participatory. It exists within a framework of passionate interchange between leader and follower, like a well-choreographed dance of ideas. Just as every CEO both leads and follows the board, the same principles of constructive interaction apply to the CEO's relationship with his followers (read: staff), even though that relationship is decidedly more hierarchical.

WHAT STYLE OF LEADERSHIP IS RIGHT FOR YOUR ORGANIZATION?

My view of leadership is rooted in what I've seen work over the long haul. Whenever I'm asked to identify the one essential quality of an effective leader, the single mandatory characteristic for anyone in a leadership position, I always come back to humility. The authentic leader, the one who inspires followers and is responsive to their needs, isn't the pulpit-thumping, boardroom-admonishing, order-barking character we've all seen in the movies or, worse, in our own organizations. The true leader has the attitude of a servant. He is the servant of the organization, its effectiveness, the necessity of its cause, and those within the organization.

That's not to say that *stylistically* a leader must always be humble. Effective leaders recognize context and adapt themselves accordingly. A good example is the former mayor of New York. When 9/11 happened, New Yorkers responded well to the authoritarian leadership style of Rudolph Giuliani, but post-crisis, when everyday city problems such as homelessness rose to the fore again, a more nuanced approach was needed, and Giuliani's tough-guy persona did poorly. Similarly, it is said that once WWII was over, the great Winston Churchill's bombast was rendered totally ineffective. Many leaders today make the mistake of trying to be a hero, instead of just leading well—with humility. You can be heroic without all the window dressing.

One such leader in the nonprofit sector was Sean McGovern. Sean interviewed for the CEO position at a large healthcare services nonprofit where I happened to be on the review committee. I discouraged him from applying because I felt we needed somebody with more "business" skills (as you'll see, I got this one colossally wrong). Sean not only got the job, he went on to an astonishing eleven-year run of fundraising leadership that grew the organization eightfold; from about 50 people to 250, with a corresponding growth in budget from $5.5 million to $44 million. His leadership style could best be described as "inquisitive," with a strong dose of humility. Sean was a master investigator who would try out ideas on people, and he always approached fundraising strategically by asking, "Where should I apply my time to get the most return for my organization?" He decided that the most lucrative activity his nonprofit could engage in was to learn everything there was to know about healthcare and the revenue attendant to it: government grants, third-party Medicaid reimbursements, and eventually private grants and private foundations. Over the course of his tenure, he essentially solved the revenue problem for his organization and he left systems in place to ensure the continued revenue growth of the organization once he left. He made himself obsolete in the best possible way—a textbook example of how to be humble and yet supremely effective.

In our nonprofit sector, an autocratic style can be devastating. As an external consultant, I was part of one particular nonprofit CEO's executive team and, over the course of five meetings, each time, without exception, he reminded the members of his executive team that their job could be on the line. What a disconnect that was; in a nonprofit, of all places. It created an atmosphere of fear and despondency. These staff members had been drawn to their mission because they were trying to be of service to the greater good; instead, they found themselves in an unforgiving pressure cooker, thanks to the out-of-context management style of the CEO. The CEO's program directors acted like frightened children. Even when they wanted to express *approval* of something, their response was inevitably, "Well, maybe, but we have to see what the executive director wants." This artificial logjam was unyielding, and although this CEO's nonprofit survives, it can only achieve greatness when and if the CEO becomes more self-aware about how his autocratic style squashes other people. People need to be empowered to make decisions within a system of checks and balances, not because they're terrified of what the executive director will think.

However, the issue of leadership style doesn't end there. When leaders align their style with the context at hand, they must also guard against a potentially devastating loss of perspective. The loss of perspective is perhaps the single greatest hazard facing today's nonprofit CEO. There's a simple test of whether or not you've lost perspective: If you absolutely need things to go a certain way, then you've lost perspective. Naturally the executive director has to *direct* strategy—it's right there in the job title. But if that direction goes awry, adjustments have to be made, not proclamations of why a failing strategy is the correct one. Not only won't it work, it will destroy any semblance of teamwork in the process.

I once heard a presentation by Warren Buffett that's remained with me ever since, and that speaks to the fundamental responsibilities of a leader. Buffett was asked what his job was when he came in every morning. Was it to look at the markets and make sure he knew what was going on? Was it to develop an acute financial analysis of that morning's economic news? None of the above, Buffett said (though I paraphrase). His job when he comes to work each morning is to support his staff. Translated for the nonprofit world, the Oracle of Omaha's message is this: The most important assets you have as a leader are the people in your organization, especially because your nonprofit is ultimately about promoting the advancement of civil society, no matter the specifics of your mission.

WHAT A FUNDRAISING LEADER DOES

I often say that the fundraising profession is a practitioner's profession as opposed to a theoretical one. Even though theory is important to us, it is not a primary driver. We're trying to get a result; namely, more philanthropy for the institutions we represent. To achieve that result, your greatest distinguishing skill as a fundraising leader will always be your ability to develop and nurture relationships. This quality of leadership requires you to be curious about people: how they express themselves, the ideas and values that attract them, and how your mission is connected to the person identified as a prospective supporter.

It is a demanding task, to say the least. Developing relationships requires a significant professional and emotional investment, which makes it both time- and energy-consuming. Couple that with the high rate of failure when asking for support and this one-two punch will easily and often knock the timid right out of the fundraising ring. Many people in the social sector are unable to mature past (in a professional sense) the disappointment of frequent rejection. They mistakenly assess their time spent cultivating donors as nonproductive. It's little wonder that so many fundraisers prefer largely impersonal fundraising avenues such as grants, since the emotional impact of rejection is mitigated by anonymity. But this is an incorrect and ultimately destructive conclusion to draw, since on further analysis, every potential revenue source has a human dimension to it, if you are open to trying to connect with it.

Consider how you last responded to a funder's request for proposal (RFP). Did you view it as an abstract set of questions that required a straightforward, nuts-and-bolts response? Or did you see the RFP as the first step toward developing a rapport with the program officer overseeing the grant? Did you call the grant officer or consider doing so? That type of proactive step is time-consuming, and still no guarantee of success, but it can and often does make the difference. You might want to see it as a chance to listen and learn about the person behind the RFP, to discover what he or she is really asking, and to understand what the donor organization wants to achieve through the grant. I'm aware that under many circumstances, this type of call may be against the funder's policies, and if that is the case, then please ignore my suggestion. But assuming you are free of such policy restrictions, doesn't it behoove you as the fundraiser-in-chief to pick up the phone and see what else you can learn about that person and his or her true needs? As fundraising practitioners, we must always remember that the results we seek are not always available on the first go-round, but every inquiry has the potential to lead us to our ultimate goal.

The Value of Listening When Fundraising

Vastly underrated in fundraising, though equal in importance to the gift of gab, is the ability to know when to listen and the willingness to do so. Here's an example of why silence can be "golden": Several years ago I sought to affirm a $100,000 gift from a businessman/ philanthropist for a program that aimed to prevent teenage pregnancies and to educate boys and girls about their roles in the unwanted pregnancy problem. The executive director and I had barely started the meeting when the philanthropist shocked us by saying, "I hope that you're also focused on abstinence." My heart sank down to my boots. Nothing in my preparatory research indicated that he would come at us from that angle. I reflexively paused and then said to him, rather haltingly, "Um, you've thought about this subject, I can see."

I thought we were already dead in the water, and what's worse, the $100,000 gift was going to either make or break this program. But a tiny little voice in my head reminded me that it is always the fundraiser's job to listen and to learn more. So I asked, "Can you tell me more?" In advance of our meeting, I had coached the executive director that if I was in dialogue with the funder, especially if any resistance was to come up, I should be the lightning rod, not her. The philanthropist told us how he thought that the best thing was for kids to wait before having sexual relations. Our hopes were crumbling by the second.

But then a long pause ensued between us, and we were able to silently resist our urge to "fill in" that awkward silence until, all on his own, the philanthropist himself said, "*But* I realize that's more of a perfect world than we live in, and a program like yours is necessary, so let me hear the details." The executive director quickly and gleefully painted in all the finer points for him, and we walked out with a $100,000 gift. So what's the moral of the story? Just as no one's ever listened himself out of a job, you can rest assured that you won't ever listen yourself out of a donation, though you might just listen yourself into one.

The Bucks Stop (and Start) Here

Of course, silence is only a small part of your arsenal as a fundraising leader. You've also got to be an inspired advocate for your organizational vision; in other words, you must be able to describe how the future will be different once your organization has succeeded in its mission. We'll discuss this topic in greater depth in Chapter 4, when focusing on higher-level thinking, but before we do, and before we look at what often gets in the way from a fundraising perspective, I want to make one important point about fundraising responsibility. The CEO is always the agency's chief fundraiser, and that role should never be delegated to other individuals, no matter how talented they are. It's similar to the way the president of the United States never relinquishes his role as commander in chief. A common misconception among nonprofits is that you can hire someone who's a trained fundraiser and then not have to worry about fundraising anymore. You do so at your own great risk.

The CEO's role is to determine and/or approve fundraising strategy and to supervise its implementation. Though there may be one or several professional fundraisers within the organization, or hired from the outside, at the end of the day the CEO is the sine qua non of the agency's fundraising program.

THE FOUR MOST COMMON ROADBLOCKS TO
SUCCESSFUL FUNDRAISING

If your organization lacks revenue, your best program ideas can't be implemented. It's as simple as that. When it comes to fundraising, I've observed four particular roadblocks that tend to arise.

The first and most prevalent of these obstacles is the taboo that surrounds asking for money in the first place. My own personal evolution as a fundraiser began within this conundrum. When I was fifteen years old, I went to a peace conference for a group called "Quakolics"—Quakers and Catholics in dialogue. Not the most elegant of monikers, I admit, but you get the idea. The thing we all had in common was that we were studying nonviolence, and I absolutely loved the experience. But about three-quarters of the way through one of our three-hour meetings, a guy in his sixties, whom I'll call Sam, walked in. Sam started to talk about money and what was needed; he asked us if we could help and if we would give. And I thought: "This is the crassest thing I've ever heard in my life. Asking people for money like that? What nerve!" Little did I know I'd find myself a fundraiser, like Sam, all these years later. In hindsight, I can see that he actually did a terrific job. He told us how much revenue he needed, explained why the money was needed, and then asked us to give. That's not taboo. It's informative!

I grew up in the Catholic Church, and once a year the monsignor would come on a verified appointment for the annual block visit; he came to listen to how our household was doing even as he picked up his "stretch gift" (aka the block collection check) in a pre-mailed envelope. It's a fabulous method. Ever wonder why the Catholic Church gets so much money? It asks for it. If you'll pardon the expression, it asks for it religiously. The word *religio* in Latin means "to bind." You're bound to something. You're not just giving money; you are connecting yourself to something large and important to you. This is one of the underlying reasons that people donate in the first place. They want to see something happen in the world, something they themselves can't do. For instance, they want to find a solution to the cholera epidemic in Haiti, but they don't have the time or energy or wherewithal to go to Port-au-Prince and solve that problem themselves. So they donate to the charity that does that work. We as fundraisers need to remember that we aren't asking questions about current or prospective donors to be invasive. We're trying to value-align them with the issues they care about. A fundraiser makes a bridge between those who have money and those who need money for a good cause.

The second most common cause of fundraiser paralysis is the fear of making a mistake. What if I offend the donor, or ask for too much money? What if my timing is wrong? Well, to paraphrase Terry Axelrod, the founder of Benevon, by the time the fundraiser asks for money, the donor should be so connected to the mission of the organization that asking becomes nothing more than "nudging the inevitable." It should be like ripe fruit dropping from a tree. In fact, a well-cultivated donor often asks: "Aren't you going to ask me for money?" There should be that level of deep engagement. That's the ideal, and it is achievable if fundraisers have done their job assiduously. Ironically, the biggest mistake most CEOs make isn't asking for money. It's *not* asking for money once they've extensively educated their donors about their organization.

A third frequent impediment to successful fundraising that bears mentioning, even when taboo and the fear of making a mistake can be overcome, is the issue of complexity. In a fiercely competitive environment, fundraisers steel themselves while they try to figure out how to get more money. But often a breakdown occurs when they enter that uncomfortable corporate office, say, or that of a government bureaucrat for a meeting. Suddenly they're faced with a steep learning curve, as cryptic acronyms are batted around the room like menacing flies. Feeling overwhelmed, the fundraiser cowers inwardly, thinking, "I just wanted to be of help. I didn't enter this field to write a government grant. I just wanted to help the homeless or make sure that dying people had respect in the last weeks of their lives." The seminal drive to do good withers against sophisticated business complications, and as a result, the fundraiser and the vast majority of nonprofits end up never getting off the dime. The way around this dilemma is surprisingly simple: Ask questions. If you don't know what to ask, you can always buy time by saying: "I'll get back to you later on that." Thousands of people have successfully completed grant applications or closed deals with corporate partners. With a bit more study time you can confidently add yourself to that list. Not knowing is forgivable; not caring enough to find out is just that.

The fourth common roadblock is an (ill-informed) acceptance of the notion that "no one wants to fund overhead, and development is overhead." While this is fundamentally a structural problem within our sector, it nonetheless arises in the individual interactions between fundraisers and donors, and therefore bears scrutiny. I believe the vast majority of nonprofits are in it for the long haul to remedy the social dilemma that they've set out to solve. That long-range vision must be reflected through leadership, particularly in the area of fundraising.

Bill Shore, the executive director of Share Our Strength, the national organization working to end childhood hunger in the United States, eloquently observes:

> *Nonprofits should be judged by their impact.... If we were able to eliminate childhood hunger in the United States in the next three years, but with an overhead of, say, 46 percent, wouldn't that be better than an anti-hunger organization with an overhead of 9 percent that never makes the slightest dent?*[2]

Whether or not you agree, overhead costs will always be an issue for your agency. If you can't find a way to speak of it directly in your fundraising endeavors, it's advisable to seek a way to connect the concept of overhead to a donor's everyday or work life. Ask donors about operating costs in their own businesses and you'll likely find people who can suddenly relate to your dilemma. Sometimes just speaking to people honestly, using examples from real life, will take you a long way. At the very least, you should explain clearly and thoughtfully what makes up your overhead costs, why the donor's support is needed to meet them, and the broad context that connects these mundane expenses with your larger mission.

Leadership requires tenacity, and fundraising leadership is no different. Fear of rejection stifles and ultimately cripples fundraising. As Tom Wolfe wrote in *The Bonfire of the Vanities*, "A frantic salesman is a dead salesman." The fear of rejection freezes fundraising efforts before they even begin, and stultifies your ability to meet your revenue goals and achieve your mission. Rather than inhibiting yourself and developing a strategy that cuts off opportunity, the trick is to embrace fear and learn to work with it. Disappointment is a part of all relationships. Remember, courage isn't an absence of fear; it's the willingness to keep trying *in spite* of it.

Embracing your fear can actually be productive. When a request for a contribution is denied, you can learn why it was denied. This information will probably teach you something about how your organization is perceived by prospective donors, plus you can possibly position yourself for the next appeal. With one foundation I applied to, I was denied for nine consecutive years, until at last on the tenth try fortune smiled upon me. Each of those nine lonely years, I would call the grant officer and process the rejection. But by the third year we were actually kibitzing on the phone. What kept the application in play—and kept me trying—was that the funder's priorities perfectly matched the program for which we sought support. Sometimes you meet the right person at the wrong time. In this case, if our values hadn't been superbly aligned, I probably would not have stuck with it.

APPLYING THE LESSONS OF LEADERSHIP

They say good fortune comes when opportunity meets preparedness. Thus, while fundraising leaders have to actually bring in revenue, they must also teach others the steps that prepare an organization to receive funds. (The Casebook at the end of this chapter will give you some idea of how you can make that happen.) Like any responsibility, the development process requires time, and too often trustees are impatient—they want results faster than can reasonably be delivered. But trustees can be taught how to think more like fundraisers.

Recognize the Value of Good Scheduling and Time Management

In practical terms, leaders are best served by scheduling time each week to focus on fundraising activities, such as developing strategy, meeting with donors, and working with the staff to support or direct the myriad activities of the development program. There are specific fundraising tasks and strategy implementations that you cannot and truly should not delegate to anyone else. It is incumbent upon you as the fundraising leader to identify what those tasks are and apply a laserlike focus in order to get them accomplished.

I readily empathize with those nonprofit executives whose reality finds them bogged down in routine administrative matters. You have little time to propel your organization's advancement, even though your judgment and authority are essential to making this happen. The leader has to be able to take advantage of opportunities for advancement, and many organizational opportunities are really fundraising opportunities. So, before we dive into tactics, let me state what ought to be obvious, but is too often neglected: A CEO without free time to fundraise is a CEO who relegates the agency's hope of raising revenue to the dustbin.

Fundraising leadership requires a regimen of actually focusing on the preset development strategy. That regimen in turn focuses on the small actions that carry out the articulated strategy. Many organizations lack this focus, jumping from one activity to another without a clear sense of how each supports the preset plan. You may discover that the plan needs to be changed; if so, change it. But until that happens, you'll be best served by following your plan rather than consigning it to the shelf.

Calendaring your development strategy often goes a long way, too. In many of the organizations where I've worked, we've achieved fine results using the Outlook scheduler to post deadlines and upcoming markers for deadlines, plus we've set internal deadlines to be sure we were getting to our goals. For example, if we knew that our holiday Thank-A-Thon (see Chapter 8 on year-end giving) needed to happen a week before Thanksgiving, say, on November 15, we didn't only mark that as the date for the phone campaign. We also marked our calendars on October 15, one month ahead, to allow time to mobilize our volunteers (we needed twenty) and to write the scripts we would use to train the volunteers. We also allocated prep time to choose which donors we wanted to call and why. You can find a sample annual fundraising calendar online at www.thenonprofitfundraisingsolution.com.

Teach Everyone to Connect the Dots Between Fundraising and Performance

I'm often discouraged to see that most donors don't know the first thing about the organizations they give to. It's incumbent upon the fundraiser to help the donor understand what the nonprofit's work entails. Furthermore, I can't overemphasize how important it is that fundraising leaders know how the money works in their organization and convey that information to donors, staff, and everyone else who will listen. That's right. Everyone in your agency should know how the money works, from the receptionist to the CEO, to each and every trustee. They may not need to have all the nitty-gritty details, but they at least have to know the basics.

Receptionists, for instance, are in contact with the entire gamut of individuals connected to your agency, from the clients who benefit from its programs to the donors whose funding makes those programs run. They should be able to explain to clients why their fee is essential to that program. They should be able to explain to visiting funders how their grant makes a real impact. That's the degree of knowledge proficiency for which your organization should aim. Unfortunately, this is rarely the case; in fact, I've had many conversations with *board members,* no less, who lacked sufficient knowledge to carry out these simple yet germane conversations.

A fundraising leader must be committed to funding the development program, especially because most development programs are woefully underfunded. How to do that is a classic catch-22: You need funds to raise funds. When it comes to fundraising, most nonprofit executives have high expectations for their fundraising strategy and tactics, but their time and money investment in fundraising borders on the abysmal. They'll sooner fund the program, then the administration, and then as an afterthought they might fund fundraising. (I'm sure my evaluation colleagues, who are experts in evaluating outcomes and measurements, would contend that they were the last ones on the chow line in terms of funding commitment, though at best we share the same paltry leftovers.)

The inability of many CEOs to connect the dots between sufficiently funding the fundraising program and enjoying the high performance they desperately seek is all too common, and from a fundraiser's standpoint, painful to behold. Unfortunately, it's this very inability to recognize the fundraising-to-performance connection that condemns an organization to forever walking in place, never able to rise above a fixed plateau of lackluster impact. So what can you do to make that connection?

Craft and Tailor Your Development Plan and Committee

Start by crafting a development plan. The development plan is written around the product that the fundraiser is selling to donors; namely, the impact that a program has on the community it serves. A good first step is to audit or review where your funding is coming from now. Then assess whether you can get more money from your current revenue sources. We'll get more into the pros and cons of revenue diversification in Chapter 4; for the moment, though, suffice it to say that any development plan needs to look as deeply as possible into existing and analogous revenue streams.

Your development committees have to be action-oriented as well. The difference between a "plain old" leader and a fundraising leader is that instead of merely inviting someone to a meeting, a fundraising leader prepares a list of people whom the invitee might know and asks, "What can you tell me about Mr. Smith? What's his business? Have you ever heard him talking about giving to us or giving to another charity? How would he be inclined to be involved with us?" You might scrutinize names of donors or prospective donors to see if any members of the committee know them. Many development committees don't even have a goal for how much money to raise, which is somewhat akin to trying to buy a house without inquiring about its price. You develop your goal by looking at the number of prospects you have, vetting them for what you think their capacity is to give, and then creating an overall goal range for the committee based on those prospects, from the low to the high end.

Every day, at most development committee meetings all over the country, trustees sit around and talk about fundraising. They'll say, "We should be submitting more grant applications," or "We should be soliciting more major donors for money or planned gifts." What's called for is a whole new approach. I suggest no committee meetings be allowed to happen until, say, five committee members have each met with one or two major donors or donor prospects. Then you can start the development committee meeting with action-oriented questions such as, "What can you tell me about your meeting with X, Y, or Z? What did we learn from the conversation? What was it like to write that grant?" You replace an orthodoxic approach— focused on getting the correct thinking—with an orthopraxic approach, focused on the practice and application of the work. As you can see, instead of talking about fundraising, your committee will be processing and learning from everyone's real-life experiences.

Calculate Your Return on Investment

Another necessary step for your development plan is to create a method of calculating the return on investment (ROI) of each aspect of your fundraising program. This requires an analysis of the time and financial resources consumed by fundraising, so you know how well your efforts are paying off. ROI is a calculation that shows the number of dollars raised compared to the amount spent. Every nonprofit that wants to know if its fundraising program is working should take this important performance measure seriously.

To determine your fundraising ROI, simply calculate "donations received" divided by "fundraising expenses." This is the standard formula. Because you want to avoid confusion when stating the ROI, I always further explain ROI by saying specifically, "We have raised X dollars for every dollar spent on our fundraising program." This keeps it simple and clearly demonstrates what you mean by ROI. So, for example, if you raised $27,000 with an expense of $4,000, your ROI was $6.75. Your report would say, "We have raised $6.75 for every dollar we spent on fundraising."[3] Bear in mind when calculating and reporting your ROI that not all return on investment is immediate. Some returns may have to be projected two or three years into the future. For instance, your return on initiatives such as a planned giving program or a leadership council (which I'll discuss in detail in Part Two) is typically deferred.

When taken together and applied to fundraising, these lessons of leadership contribute not only to a better understanding of how the money in your organization works, but also to a readily transmittable package of concrete information that will better train your staff and make a lasting impression on your donors and trustees.

HOW TO KNOW IF YOUR LEADERSHIP IS WORKING

Is there a way to know if your leadership is truly working? A good barometer of effectiveness is encapsulated by the answers to these simple questions: Do you have a better set of problems today than you had yesterday? Or last week? Or last month or year? You will know you are truly leading when you can answer "yes."

Leadership is results-driven, and if your organization is moving in the right direction and your challenges are materializing anew instead of recurring yet again, you'll know you have the wind at your back. Of course, this may not have much to do with my father's rotting fish, but I'm sure he would agree it makes all the difference between swimming toward greatness and endlessly treading water.

CASEBOOK

Your staff can get you where you need to go only if the leader actively creates fundraising readiness. That means a cohesive, committed, and productive work environment in which the CEO shares the vision and inculcates the staff with an understanding of the values and the mission of your organization. When I was hired as the CEO of a social services nonprofit a number of years ago, I soon reached the conclusion that to be a credible leader, I needed to understand how my staff members performed their work and how they perceived the organization. But how could I gain that knowledge without arousing suspicion and otherwise disrupting our daily work? Believing that an outside eye might be more perceptive, I hired Mario Guella as a consultant to survey my staff. That decision turned out to be a seminal moment in my management of that organization, and it continues to influence my thinking to this day about leadership and its importance to fundraising.

An anonymous twenty-question paper survey revealed that many of the thirty-five staff members, having been hired to provide a specific service, had only a limited knowledge of the history, values, and mission of the organization. This ignorance was not their fault; it was due to a lack of leadership on my part. Consequently, Mario did more than simply identify the problem; he created a program to fix it by designing a series of five training sessions, each lasting two hours, to educate the staff about the organization's place in the community it served and how we intended to achieve the mission of our agency within that community. It worked brilliantly.

Mario prepared staff members to articulate a concise, sixty-second profile of the organization. This "elevator speech" was designed to succinctly communicate our organization's essence in literally the time it would take to move between ten floors on an elevator. The message was further tailored to engage all potential listeners, from those completely unfamiliar with the organization to those who knew something about it. It didn't take long to see that an informed and enthusiastic staff is the best advertisement for any organization; in this case, by creating a small army of informed advocates, the training program simultaneously amplified my own voice as that organization's leader.

Another training session Mario designed revisited day-to-day life within the organization and how we could best work together as a team. Unlike the board and executive leadership, who have a long-range view of the organization, staff members typically have a short(er)-term view focused on daily operations and therefore limited in scope. So, at the third session, Mario had us read the vision statement, which described what the future would look like once we'd succeeded in our mission. He then asked questions designed to spur discussion: Does it inspire you? Is it realistic? Do you think our clients believe it? A board member and I then described how the vision statement was created. This one exercise created so much positive energy that I believe it powered our upward progress over the next three years.

A subsequent session asked a board member to describe the work of the board. Mario facilitated a deeper conversation not only to provide a taste of what the board did for the agency, but equally important, to demonstrate the humanity of the "big, bad board members." Staff members gained a greater understanding of the board's essential work, and for many of them, it was the first time they even realized we had a board.

The final session sought to instill an understanding of how the staff supports the leadership by having everyone in the room address the question: "Is it lonely at the top?" The frankness of people's answers, and the bonds that they created among us, provided a natural and elegant conclusion to the program. I was pleasantly surprised at how impactful Mario's program was. It helped us create a confident organization, with a clear understanding of itself and a focus on using its cumulative expertise to support the mission of what was perceived as *our* organization. Mario and I had worked together behind the scenes to create the program, but had I tried to deliver the training without his help, it would have been a mistake. External facilitation can sometimes carry the day, and help bring about renewed strength and faith in your leadership.

AT THE END OF THE DAY

Leadership may begin at the top, but it extends throughout your organization. The better informed everyone is about how the money works in your organization, the more "fundraising ready" you will be. A real development plan sets a great foundation, and knowing your ROI is essential. Ask yourself if you have a better set of problems today than you had yesterday.

CHAPTER THREE

TUNING UP THE BOARD FOR EFFECTIVE FUNDRAISING PERFORMANCE

THE INNER SANCTUM OF AURELIA'S board at Caring Hospice, Inc. has been my private observatory for more than a decade. I have witnessed nothing less than an organizational miracle within its confines. Caring Hospice is a nonprofit that trains and supports hospital chaplains. When I first began observing the board, Aurelia was new to the executive director post, and though this was only her third executive position, she took on the mighty task of transforming the board. What had been a stodgy healthcare and pastoral care agency is now a thought leader in its field and a national beacon in palliative care.

Before Aurelia's arrival, the board was mired in the past. You'd often see trustees disdainfully roll their eyes whenever any sort of innovation was brought up for discussion, and say, "Well, we've never done it that way before!" The two founding coexecutive directors had actually done a stellar job in getting the organization to where it was when Aurelia was appointed, but the board was essentially following them without exerting leadership itself. The board members had figured out their governance structures (officer's roles, committees, design, operational policies, meeting schedule and protocols), which is no small feat, but no one on the board was leading Caring Hospice in figuring out how to get bigger and better. This issue grew to dramatic proportions because, over the course of twenty years, the healthcare industry had literally revolutionized itself, and Caring Hospice—with its same narrow mission—risked being left behind, and missing a gigantic opportunity for increased funding and growth. While it used to be that no one wanted to talk about death and dying, over the course of two decades, palliative care was finally having its moment in the sun.

I've watched Aurelia's board transformation closely, from a body that followed the lead of the two cofounders into a partnership between her and her board members. Previously, revenues were entirely dependent on fees from the hospitals that Caring Hospice contracted with for chaplain services. Now the board members are mostly corporate executives (an intentional recruitment strategy, as you shall see) who, by the end of that transformation period, have become fundraisers in their own right, and the board's core strength has evolved into securing extremely lucrative corporate partnerships. Getting the board to its current level of success was a messy process, to put it generously. Trustees had to be transitioned off the board and hurt feelings were plentiful. But the board never lost sight that the transition was the best thing for the organization. Today, its work is unrecognizable, in the best sense of the word, from what it was ten years ago.

In this chapter, we'll examine the following issues from a fundraiser's perspective:

- Why the relationship between the board and its executive is so critical
- How to have a shared vision for the future, and why that "forward-looking" capacity will raise more money
- How to identify and add to the core strengths of the board
- How to recruit and retain good trustees
- How the board can oversee fundraising performance, even if fundraising is not its primary strength
- How to ascertain and boost the giving commitment of each trustee through my "gift of significance" approach

Giving the board support and tending to its management is a particularly challenging aspect of the executive director's job because of an inconsistency. On the one hand, the executive director (ED) works for the board; on the other, the same executive plays a significant role in developing the best board possible. My colleague Alex Plinio, codirector of the Rutgers Business School's Institute for Ethical Leadership, is fond of saying that "an executive director gets the board that he or she deserves."[1] While I endorse this sentiment, I would add that you don't have to settle for mediocrity. You can improve your current board by giving it a proper tune-up.

THE CRITICAL RELATIONSHIP BETWEEN AN ORGANIZATION'S CEO AND ITS BOARD

In my first nonprofit CEO position, at an agency that served the homeless, I effectively forgot about the board. Chalk it up to inexperience, but I didn't yet understand how the board could make me a more effective executive, or how we could boost the success of our organization by learning to work together. While I met all the technical requirements and complied with the due process responsibilities, in my heart I felt the board was mostly a nuisance with its "three duties."[2] It was only later, with experience and professional maturity (and the help of a good coach), that I was able to recognize my error. Most important, I learned how to avoid making it again, just as you may if you have a similar challenge. Ironically, in looking back on that experience now, I see how much there was to recommend about that board and its members: They were relentless in their love of the mission and forward thinking about expanding to meet our clients' needs. One of them, a young attorney who was our board chair, even went on to become the state's governor and later a U.S. senator. Clearly, in this instance, I let gold dust slip right through my fingers.

Back when I started in the sector, there were very few graduate nonprofit management programs for people working in the public interest. The expansion of these programs and the greater availability of nonprofit resources have professionalized the field. As Michael Davidson, an experienced board coach with whom I have worked on several assignments, says, "We no longer see as many organizations run by a charismatic leader who does everything. Today's EDs are looking for the board to be their partner."

The relationship between the CEO and the board is the foundation of a dynamic organization.[3] In America, the very concept of a board of directors harkens all the way back to the Puritans at the time of the Massachusetts Bay Company. Among other things, a board was conceived to fulfill the desire for centralized governance coupled with some measure of executive oversight. The stubborn persistence of these desires and the power of a board of directors are possibly why the board concept endures to this day. A board can literally transform an organization, in part by choosing an executive who, as management author Jim Collins notes, "is selfless, who approaches challenges with a workman-like diligence, and who is, without qualification, committed to the mission and future success of the organization he or she leads."[4] In other words, a well-chosen executive can work with the board to take their nonprofit to the next echelon of mission service and fundraising success. And yet, although the board chooses the executive director, the best executive directors understand that they get the board that they in turn create. It's a paradox, to be sure, almost like babysitting an older sibling. The executive director has to train and guide the board to become strong, functional, strategic, and collegial—even as the executive works for that board. Cultivating an engaged and forward-thinking board doesn't just support the organizational vision, though; it literally guides that vision toward its full realization.

Some nonprofit CEOs may feel awkward about "bossing" the boss. Others, recognizing that the board is not firing on all cylinders, tune out. They sit back and glare angrily at board meetings and mark time until a new job offer is received, or perhaps they count the days until retirement. In order to align their visions, the executive and the board must often work through the differences they have. And work through them they must, because without such alignment, no organization will ever move forward as successfully as it could. It is therefore incumbent upon all parties to cultivate this special and determinant relationship.

ALIGNMENT OF VISION THROUGH DEEPER INQUIRY

What do we mean when we say that the CEO's and the board's visions are aligned? It's not as though one day, as if by magic, they suddenly begin to march in lockstep. By one measure, we could say that a board and CEO are aligned when they can both agree on a five-year plan, or agree when annual reviews of both the CEO and the trustees should happen. We could even say that the "grand-daddy" of alignment is when your organization is accomplishing its mission. But the concept of alignment is probably best understood by examining the processes it takes to achieve alignment.

In everyday life, when you take your car in to have its wheels aligned, you are doing so to get better performance. Specifically, you want the tires to wear more evenly so that they don't just consume the edge or the center. If they wear evenly across the tire, you can get an extra 15,000 to 20,000 miles on them. You also want the car to hold the road at the center, as opposed to veering right or left, so the driver doesn't have to oversteer. That contributes to safety. So you align for less wear and tear, —better performance— and safety.

When we put our nonprofits up on the proverbial "lift," we are looking for a similar sort of nimbleness. The way to acquire it is to have a real strategic plan in place, with community and client input, so your trustees understand your thinking about where you want the organization to go. You then want to meet with the board, go over the plan, and create a depth of understanding and action around that plan. Too often, strategic plans sit on the shelf without anyone ever looking at them, and many of the most important questions, first framed by Peter Drucker, go unasked. Who is your customer? What does the customer want and need? Who are your partners and what do they want? What is high performance? What is optimal service?[5]

In the old TV series *Columbo,* after everyone had said their piece about whatever criminal case was in play, Lieutenant Columbo (played by Peter Falk) would almost always do the same thing before walking out the door. He'd stop in the doorway, look back into the room, and say, "Just one more thing," or "There's something that bothers me." He took every inquiry and pushed it one step deeper. For my money, Columbo is about as good as it gets as a model of what the CEO and the board need to be aligned around, which is the notion of deeper inquiry. Not to solve crimes, of course, but to uncover new ways to innovate.

IDENTIFYING AND ADDING TO YOUR BOARD'S CORE STRENGTH

Most boards have one dominant core strength—something that comes to them easily, like events planning or networking. But for your board to help raise your organization to the next level, you need to expand beyond your core strength.

Development of these new strengths must reflect what your board needs or desires to excel at, and it's not necessarily what comes naturally to the board. For instance, your board may wish to develop a new strength in long-term planning or how to start a quality assurance program. New core strengths can be tough to generate, but their importance in galvanizing and directing fundraising energy can't be overstated. As the inimitable Yogi Berra once put it, "If you don't know where you're going, you'll wind up someplace else."

Core strengths come in many shapes and sizes. Some boards are strong on compliance. They know that their conduct is congruent with their bylaws and any other rules and regulations they've adopted. Others are strong in their sensitivity to the clients they serve. They regularly ask themselves, "Are we helping them and doing well by them?" Some boards are glued together by prestige; trustees enjoy belonging to the organization and want to be affiliated with it as people of influence. Still others may be especially strong at fundraising, long-range planning, strategic thinking, or program evaluation. The list goes on and on.

Determining a board's core strength can usually be done by reviewing past minutes, attending some board meetings, and having a few conversations with key trustees. The dominant driver will inevitably become apparent. You may even feel you already have an intuitive sense of your board's core strength just while reading these characterizations. If not, there are analytically oriented assessment tools available to help you figure it out. The national nonprofit Board Source developed one such tool called "the Board Self-Assessment."[6] This self-assessment allows your board members to candidly reflect on how well the board is meeting its governance responsibilities. Once the assessment is complete, you will have the basis for setting priorities, developing core strengths, and motivating your board members—individually and collectively—to strengthen their performance and governance practices.

However, as attractive as some types of board strengths may sound, no CEO should simply announce something like "our board needs to become more comfortable with external affairs." (External affairs is understood in the nonprofit world to be synonymous with fundraising.) As we shall see, there needs to be a valid reason for developing a new core strength beyond just wishful thinking. Let's return for a moment to the story of Aurelia's board at Caring Hospice for an example.

Why would Aurelia think Caring Hospice could develop a new core strength in corporate partnerships? Even though palliative care was now out in the open, corporate giving was (and is still) only about 5 percent of the nearly $300 billion coming into U.S. nonprofits every year.[7] Hardly a treasure awaiting easy plunder.

But Aurelia found a valid reason within herself. She astutely recognized that many of the corporate executives she was connected to had experienced death and dying issues, and so her first innovation in tuning up her board was to recruit trustees who could advocate for Caring Hospice from within their corporations. Most nonprofits appeal to a corporation without having an insider shepherding their support request; she knew that she could vastly improve her chances of securing some of that 5 percent if she had her own insiders on her board.

But her board's new core strengths go even further than corporate partnerships; they are now bona fide thought leaders in the hospice industry. Aurelia wanted a thought-leading board—though here, too, she didn't make that decision randomly. She chose that additional core strength after she did a survey of different types of boards and got to know several other executive directors, whom she asked: "What do you think is your board's natural strength? And what would you want it to be if you could wave a magic wand?" She realized that among her peers, there were very few thought leaders in her field, and she understood that the corporate contacts she had could provide this value. They were strategists. They were thinking people. So she headed in that direction. Through careful recruitment, which we'll discuss momentarily, and a commitment to learning as much about her industry as possible, Aurelia created a board of solid leaders who now speak as ambassadors for the organization, and who think as much as she does about the strategic issues they will face in the coming decade.

The American Canyon Society (first mentioned in Chapter 1) is another case in point. The ACS board was made up of scientists whose natural strengths were research and deep thinking. But the core strength they developed was turning themselves into fundraisers. This is not to say that every board has the skills or interest to lead the fundraising program of a nonprofit. I think it's more accurate to think of your board as the mechanic, whose job is to make sure that the fundraising engine is working properly. To be effective, a board must rely on its natural and core strengths first, and understand in what way it can best lead and align those strengths with the organization's needs.

Surprised? Does this sound like heresy coming from a fundraiser? After all, shouldn't all boards be fundraising leaders? I don't believe there is one set model into which all boards must fit; however, when board members truly understand their collective role, and function as a team, they *inevitably* raise more money.

What If Your Board's Core Strength Isn't Fundraising?

Suppose you determine that your board's core strength isn't fundraising. What steps can the board take to ensure this essential function is still properly carried out? Here are several actions you should take, in their ideal order of execution:

1. *Recruit a fundraising professional for the board.* A value-based fundraiser, who knows how to cultivate the right revenue source for the unique mission and culture of a nonprofit, is an invaluable asset to have on any board. To readily find one, I suggest you attend conferences, such as those organized by the Association of Fundraising Professionals (AFP). The AFP hosts hundreds of conferences in every rural and urban region of the country. (Details about locating your regional AFP chapter and their lists of meetings, seminars, and conferences are available at www.afpnet.org.)

2. *Put a development/fundraising plan in place.* The development plan itemizes each area of your current and prospective revenues, and lets you know how you're doing and what areas can be improved. It also analyzes return on investment (ROI) for each revenue area, which is part of preparing your annual ROI (which will be discussed shortly).

3. *Establish gift acceptance policies and use them.* Typically these policies are written by a consultant or a professional fundraising staff person and approved by the board. Gift acceptance tends to go astray either because of an absence of a policy or because, sadly, policies don't get read until a controversial issue arises, at which point one often hears board members say, "Well, we never signed off on this type of gift!" Gift acceptance policies can be as short as five pages with fifteen to twenty policies, though they are usually more in the range of twenty-five pages with a hundred policies.

4. *Develop the necessary committee structure.* This is an essential step in tuning up any board. At minimum you need to have an overall development committee; usually a planned giving committee and an events committee may also make sense, but they are sometimes structured as subcommittees of the development committee.

5. *Prepare an annual ROI report.* Using the return on investment approach to analyze fundraising performance is an excellent way to engage leadership and staff on how best to plan your future fundraising activities. You will find that board members who have for-profit business experience will likely be able to help with such an approach to planning and resource allocation, although these days there are plenty of good graduates of nonprofit management programs who also have these skills.[8]

6. *Direct volunteers toward fundraising activity.* Whatever item is on the agenda, your board members must learn to ask what that activity's underlying fundraising component is and then consider the skills and interests they need to bring to each activity. What kinds of fundraising *might* the board members be good at? The affable, outgoing member—the one you would most like to have a cup of coffee with—might be terrific at asking people for money. This person could be chair of the major gifts committee. The quiet, bookish member who would never dream of asking a donor for money might have good written communication skills. That's someone who could write reports and appeal letters, or review the materials produced by the development office once or twice a year and offer a fresh point of view. The detail-oriented, mathematically inclined member, the one who always seems

to have a calculator in hand, is likely to be a whiz at reviewing budgets. Of course I'm stereotyping here, but my point is that each board member's board assignment should be in line with the individual's skills and talents, and those talents can in turn be repurposed for fundraising. If you are unsure of what focus certain board members have, ask them. Have someone from your nominating committee join the conversation and review the various ways your organization works and raises money with each board member. Ask board members what role they would prefer to play. Each member will likely have strong preferences, and may well appreciate such focused, personal attention.

Step 1, recruiting one or more fundraising professionals to the board, merits a more expansive discussion, as it will make board oversight of the fundraising function vastly more effective. Given their pedigree, fundraising professionals are ideal candidates to supervise all of the subsequent steps on the board's behalf. Whatever the particular core strength of a board, there should always be at least one space reserved for a professional fundraiser. It's counterproductive and, frankly, a bit baffling that so many nonprofits have filled their boards with lawyers yet include no professional fundraisers. Their omission is pervasive, perhaps because most board members are unaware that fundraising is a well-established profession with tried-and-true methods and standards. Though legal skills are invaluable and certainly contribute to the success of the board, you can't hope to litigate your way to the next level of mission success. If the board consists of, say, lawyers, social workers, and business professionals, then why not recruit a fundraising and/or marketing professional who may possess skills that the board may be missing?

It would be hard to imagine leaving lawyers or business leaders off of your board, but the same pride of place should be reserved on your board for fundraising expertise. It's an essential part of nonprofit operations, and if it's not yet been allotted for, then a slot should be reserved and filled through recruitment. The chairperson of the board committee is responsible for nominating new members and should lead the recruitment effort, but don't wait for this person to act. If the chair needs support and guidance, the executive or other leading trustees have to step up and offer to help. One final caveat: Be careful not to underestimate how much time it will take to bring on new board members. Change takes time. When done well, it still takes about six to twelve months to welcome a new class of trustees to a board.

What If Your Board's Core Strength Is Fundraising?

Fundraising has become a very specialized field, and there are many fundraisers who have nuanced expertise. If you identify fundraising as your board's core strength, the next step is to reexamine your fundraising methods and identify which one(s) work best. No board is superb in all aspects of fundraising. Before we tackle the questions of trustee recruitment and retention, here are some methods your board might benefit from, even if it has a fundraising track record:

- *Campaign more.* It's perfectly fine to operate multiple campaigns at the same time.
- *Explore comprehensive giving with your top donors.* The annual gift, the stretch gift, and the planned gift should be defined and considered as a whole (see Chapter 12, on major campaigns, for a full explanation).
- *Review your development plan and address a longer period of growth over ten to twenty-five years.* Your fundraising strength can allow you to plan longer term and identify new opportunities in areas such as planned giving.
- *Execute more detailed business planning.* Business planning at this stage of development is more necessary than ever because your work is more nuanced and intricate. More detailed planning will allow you to communicate more information to your donors. Donors at higher levels of giving usually want a higher level of detail.
- *Go deeper into one dominant source of revenue and a minor revenue source.* Diversification of revenue may not be the best approach anymore; a more lucrative strategy may be looking deeper into existing revenue sources (a much deeper discussion ensues in Chapter 4).
- *Develop subcommittees that report to the main development committee.* Subcommittees help apportion resources and act as a task force to focus on specific areas of fundraising.
- *Ensure that strong connections are created between all your various fundraising tactics.* For instance, the events program

must be coordinated with the individual giving program; the individual program must be coordinated with the planned giving program. When in campaign mode, literally all fundraising needs to be coordinated with the campaign work.

- *Make routine use of external consultants to infuse your organization with higher-level talent.* Specialists with fresh perspectives can identify problems as well as previously unseen opportunities.

RECRUITING AND RETAINING GOOD BOARD MEMBERS

So how should you recruit and retain new trustees for your board? Our friend Aurelia's organization, Caring Hospice, was methodical in its approach to reshaping the board. To the great surprise of her departing predecessors, Aurelia initially asked them to attend about half of the monthly board meetings with her. Her purpose was to get their take on what was going on internally, and also to convey to the board that the process they were undergoing was a transition, not a coup d'état. As Aurelia and her predecessors debriefed, they wisely began with an assessment of the kinds of people and skill sets they were missing and thus needed to recruit and retain. Aurelia also did copious research, using wealth profiles and relational charts (which are available with software like Blackbaud) to run grids on how people were connected (e.g., Jonathan knows Susan who knows Daniel, and so on). She also reached out to everyone she knew to see who those people knew in turn.

What You Should Look for in a New Trustee

Whenever I would ask Aurelia what she looked for in a new trustee, she would say, "While interviewing the trustee candidates, each [person] must demonstrate that he or she can listen, carry responsibility, think deeply and creatively, and work as a team player. Just because they have been a captain of industry does not mean they will be right for our board."

Based on what you learn about candidates in an interview, you have to consider whether they are a good fit for your organization.

If so, where do their skills, talents, and personality fit best? Do they know how to read a financial statement? If not, what steps can be taken for them to learn? Are they open to personal giving, soliciting funds, and/or cultivating others to give? Will they open doors for you in the community? If so, how often, how many, and which doors?

They must also be asked about any conflicts of interest in putting your agency's mission first, and whether there is any possible business they're involved in that would cause them to recuse themselves from a board decision. Have they ever had an ethical breach that involved the law? If so, it shouldn't necessarily be a barrier to enrollment. In fact, it may unexpectedly be the type of life experience that makes them well suited for your board, such as if your mission is to advocate for those in jails and prisons.

Establishing Your Board's Missing Skill Sets

When establishing skill sets for a board, the governance committee, along with the CEO, typically comes up with a recruitment profile of the skills being sought, such as fundraising skills or any particular areas of expertise. Perhaps you need one or more attorneys, or former legislators, or current government officials, or someone with a design or building background.

Here are several suggestions that may facilitate new trustee selection and help you attract the best candidates:

- *Seek out members you think will be truly active.* You want passionate individuals who will enthusiastically use their experience and skill sets, not just show up occasionally for a meeting.
- *Fill your board with people who reflect the diversity of the community you serve.* Ethnicity, gender, sexual orientation, and life experience are but a few factors to consider. You want to build a connection with your constituents through your board as well.
- *Establish a clear board recruitment process.* The process should define the specific steps of how new trustees are brought on.
- *Articulate clear job descriptions and job duties.* There should be clarity as to who does what and what's expected, including meeting requirements and information about committee

assignments. You need to create a board orientation manual that allows you to share foundational documents with new trustees, such as bylaws, trustee contact information, a copy of the directors and officers liability insurance, a sample general support grant, and the strategic plan.

- *Clearly define the roles of your board members.* At minimum, you should include (and if missing, recruit for) a president, treasurer, and secretary.
- *Establish the board governance or nominating committee.* The work of such a committee is to love and nurture the team called "the board." It is also the committee's job to nominate the next class of trustees (usually three to six members) by vetting the best prospects.

I once had the pleasure of working with a board that was made up entirely of pastors. Though they were raised in the Catholic Church, perhaps the greatest fundraising organization of all time, the "blessing" of fundraising knowledge hadn't wended its way down to their particular nonprofit. They were wonderful people and had lots of planning skills, but their board needed trustees with financial and marketing expertise, too.

I met with David LaGreca of VCG Governance Matters, a New York technical assistance provider and seasoned board coach, and together we delivered a one-page profile of the board as well as a one-page description of what talent sets were still needed. A board profile is a document that describes the current demographics on the board, including the age range of the trustees as well as their business affiliations. It also gives some assessment of the board's philanthropic inclinations, their total annual giving, the highest gift ever received from any individual board member, and so on. It may also describe what a typical board meeting looks like, or its agenda. Whatever describes the temperament, culture, and behavior of the board should be in that profile.

A description of talent sets is literally just that. It can say something along these lines: "We've reviewed our current board members and we are well represented in the legal and accounting fields, but we have no one from marketing, fundraising, or communications, so those should be the main focuses of recruitment. Additionally, we always welcome knowledge experts in our field of homelessness [or blindness remediation, or housing, or another social service]."

As you begin to identify and reach out to your prospective trustees, you'll be well advised to send them out a copy of your "board book," which is a compilation of the executive director's report, current financials, any legal documents that the board should be aware of, proposed partnerships, and any reports from the staff that are of interest to the board. It's an excellent way of informing candidates of some of what is expected of them. New trustees should know they'll get the board book a week before the board meeting.

To give you one idea of how good recruitment can transform your board, in the case of the pastors, VCG interviewed our board as a group and then presented six candidates, three of whom were eventually welcomed. Thanks in large part to the missing skills those board members filled in (coupled with a leadership council, discussed in the Chapter 10 Casebook), the nonprofit went from having $54 (not a typo) in the bank to closing its books twenty-one years later with a $44 million annual budget.

You will find a sample board recruitment grid at www.thenonprofitfundraisingsolution.com.

Retention Is Crucial

Now that you've got the board you want and deserve (and here I'd like to take a moment to congratulate you), another crucial element to address is the retention of trustees who have contributed positively. Studies show that the board members who stay on the longest and see their role as contributing to its advancement are those most engaged with your mission.[9] Boards that discuss long-range plans that actually solve the social problem that the agency was founded to solve often have the highest and best retention of their trustees, not to mention the largest philanthropy from those same trustees.

It's also important that you thank (often) and recognize your board. One effective and established way is to give out awards at board meetings to recognize recent actions taken. Your trustees are far more likely to stick around if they feel their efforts are acknowledged, especially in a public forum of their peers and people they respect. Generally speaking, no one wants to toil in obscurity, least of all volunteers who receive no remuneration for their efforts. Equally important is that your trustees actually *live* the work. They need to have met clients or seen the consequences of what happens if or when your mission fails. Bringing staff and clients to board meetings from time to time, or having consumer representatives on your board, are excellent ways to make this happen.

Another noteworthy component of retention is good oversight. Every board needs to have someone whose primary task is to look after the viability of the board itself. This person's chief strength should be to facilitate teamwork. The individual filling this role is often installed as vice president and is the person who reminds the other board members of their duties and responsibilities. "How are your committee meetings?" the VP might ask, following up with additional questions such as: "Are you pleased with how things are going?" "How do you intend to make your annual gift this year, and can you make a stretch gift?" "We've only had four meetings this year and you missed three of them. Can we talk about that?"

The four keys to trustee retention can be reduced to this fairly simple mnemonic: mission success, recognition, involvement, and oversight. But what should you do if, say, a trustee decides to leave midterm? I believe your standard practice should be to immediately conduct an exit interview to learn what happened and then report this information back to the whole board. Reporting back is especially important because it subtly sends the message to the other trustees that their membership is just as important. I have been on boards where trustees have resigned and the remaining members were never told why the member left. The effect was dispiriting, to say the least. You don't want your trustees wondering if anyone will miss them when the time comes for them to leave. So, in the event of trustee attrition, honesty and an additional dose of appreciation for the remaining members will go a long way toward stanching the bleeding and avoiding any further losses.

FUNDRAISING THROUGH THE BOARD'S TRUSTEES

As we mentioned at the outset, a tuned-up board can have an absolutely transformative effect on a nonprofit. But no board tune-up would be complete without a review of, and an increase in fundraising from, the board members themselves.

Intentional Conversations

It is important to remember that even while donning their governance hats, board members are also donors. Many boards have "Give and Get" policies, whereby they define what the expected level of personal giving is from board members and what the expectation is to get support from friends, family, and other associates. I am not against having such policies; they just shouldn't be relied upon completely. I much prefer face-to-face, intentional conversations with individual trustees at least once a year, to uncover their passion for giving and any needs they may have for tax-efficient giving. The underlying tone of a Give and Get policy is often mistakenly perceived as "give, get, or get off!" Get off the board, that is. Advanced fundraising always seeks to know the donor well and respond to the donor's desire to use his or her resources toward the greatest impact. A general Give and Get policy can't reach that level of donor/trustee engagement. It may be the case that Give and Get, combined with personal attention to the donor, is the best strategy for your agency, though if you have to choose between them, opting for the intentional conversation is highly recommended.[10]

Ask for a Gift of Significance

When board members truly "get" what your organization is doing, love it as much as you do, and have the capacity to give more, it is time to ask them for a gift of significance. In preparing for such conversations, I suggest you calculate meticulously what you consider to be a gift of significance from each board member (you'll see how to specifically do so in a moment). This calculation should combine the demonstrated giving of each board member as an individual with what you believe may be the person's inclination to give more. Contrast this approach with a Give and Get policy that requires each member to contribute an identical amount, say, $10,000, and then raise another fixed amount from family and other associates. In the Give and Get approach, such prescribed amounts may be too high for some members and/or too low for others, since these policies aren't based on any real consideration of the giving or fundraising potential of the board as a diverse group of individuals. So take the time to prepare yourself empirically.

To succeed, it's vitally important that you connect the organizational mission and goals to the requirement of financial commitment. Prospective members should have well-articulated and convincing reasons for wanting to serve on the board, and the expectations of board members' personal financial commitment ought to be explicit, too. I would urge you to have the agreement memorialized in writing as well, though it's best to keep it simple. This is especially true for articulating your board members' roles as fundraisers or donors. The idea is to present board participation as an *investment* in the furtherance of the organization. This way, prospective members get a clearer understanding of the relationship between their efforts and the ability of the nonprofit to fulfill its mission. For example, "We are raising $125,000 to build more Little League fields and we have secured $25,000 from one trustee so far. We were wondering, if you joined the board, how might you see yourself giving to such a need?" Then, as we discussed in Chapter 2, sit back and listen carefully.

Past, Highest, Cumulative, and Potential Giving from Your Trustees

I've developed a methodology for calculating a gift of significance from each of your trustees, which you'll see in Figure 3-1. It begins by calculating the total giving a trustee has made over the past few years, or for as long as you have the individual's donor history. This step alone can have profound positive repercussions, because when donors are informed of the cumulative amount they've given, they are usually pleasantly surprised and proud. Even better, you have an optimal moment to drive home to your trustees how they've shown leadership, and to express your gratitude for the support they've given. Even if a trustee has no giving history, you can share the story of another trustee (with or without attribution) and suggest it as a role for others to grow into.

Subsequent to calculating cumulative giving, you'll want to then identify the largest single annual gift that person's ever made. Why? The largest single gift in a person's history indicates giving potential

Figure 3-1. Steps for calculating a gift of significance.

As a fundraiser, when you prepare to meet with a donor to ask for a gift of significance, have a donation number or range in mind that will feel right to the donor (a range is usually more effective). It is often difficult for fundraisers to come to the right number, but over the years I have found that this seven-step method helps to zero in on a target gift range.

Step 1: Calculate the person's total giving to your agency using your donor history records. If individuals have no donor history, then use the average of your overall donor giving as a possible benchmark. Sharing the donor's cumulative giving is magical because donors are not usually aware of their giving total and upon hearing it they are pleasantly surprised.

> **Step 1a:** If the donor is a trustee, have a total board giving number at the ready (i.e., a total for the year or the past two years) because that will be an important benchmark to share. If the board has no giving history, construct a goal based on your assessment of each member's individual potential to give and share that number.

Step 2: Document the amount of the donor's largest individual gift. This singular gift usually demonstrates the donor's potential to give. In rare exceptions, some largest gifts are a fluke. ("My Aunt Matilda died and left me her estate, and I gave it to you.") But usually the largest individual past gift is an indicator of a person's capacity to give more.

Step 3: Add the amount of the donor's largest gift to the average total giving. It's a number that may indicate the donor's ability to stretch to a special larger gift.

Step 4: Increase the total amount of the donor's highest gift by 50 percent to ascertain that level of possible giving.

Step 5: Secure the informal rating of peers or colleagues, if possible, concerning the donor's inclination to give and at what level.

Step 6: Research the donor's past giving to other charitable causes and note the range of those gifts.

Step 7: Examine the various numbers you generated in steps 3 through 6. Use these ratings to determine the range of giving that you are prepared to ask the donor to contribute. In most cases, a donor's giving history should carry the most weight, followed by the informal rating, and lastly, the person's past giving to other organizations.

Example:

Mr. and Mrs. Jones gave a total of $5,500 over five years. Their average gift was $1,100 ($5,500 ÷ 5 = $1,100 per year average). They were not trustees.

Their largest single gift was $1,500. Two of their peers (with whom I consulted) said, "They are very generous at their church and they also give to another nonprofit," but neither party knew their giving ranges. I ran a wealth profile on the Joneses and discovered that they had been giving at the $5,000 level to another charity. Now I had three numbers with which to work: $1,100 (average gift); $1,500 (highest gift); $5,000 (other giving to another nonprofit). Plus, I had the testimony of their peers. When I went to meet with Mr. and Mrs. Jones to ask for their support, I had in mind a range from $1,500 to $5,000; in this case, however, because I was influenced by their friends' testimony, I decided not to ask for a range but to ask simply for $5,000 and to learn more from their reaction. I could always go lower. I decided to exceed the 50 percent increase calculation noted in Step 4 based upon the peers' rating of the Joneses.

---

and sheds light on the circumstances that moved the person to make that contribution. This is a useful way to understand the values and motivations of the individual donor. Consider Nathan, age 42, who made his largest gift two years ago. Nathan is a trustee for a youth organization whose programs are all about sports as a team-learning experience. The donor database says that he made the gift because he wanted one of the ball fields reseeded and repaired. The gift was twenty-five times larger than his regular giving. From this narrative, we know that Nathan is open to capital projects and quite possibly has the capacity to give at that level again.

In other cases, you may learn that the largest gift was a fluke. Take Dominica Rose, who was a trustee of a domestic-violence prevention agency for six years. Her largest gift was fifteen times greater than any other gift she'd made, but it turned out that she donated from income that she had received as an inheritance. Thus, a repeat gift of that magnitude was, understandably, out of the question for her. Her large gift was simply an act of true philanthropy, the living out of the actual meaning of the word, which is "love for fellow man."

Another important metric to have at the ready is the total board giving over the past year or two. This figure not only intrigues trustees, it provides an easy way to derive a benchmark for giving. You simply divide the number of trustees by the total giving to calculate the average board gift. A word of caution, though: The Pareto principle, also known as the 80/20 rule, applies in this case, because approximately 80 percent of your revenue usually comes from only 20 percent of your funders. (Since the 2008 recession, the 80/20 rule has often been the 90/10 rule.) The average is therefore a guideline, but should not be the basis for each of your "asks."

What to Do If Past Board Giving Is Poor?

Suppose you not only need to augment your board's giving, you have to reverse a period of unimpressive or downright inadequate donations. Obviously, the last thing you want to do is suggest that this uninspired giving continue. One possible way out is to construct a goal based on your assessment of the board members' *potential* to give, which you would then share with them. That goal is best stated as a range, say, from $50,000 to $65,000, though you'll want to be honest and explain to trustees that even though it's based on factual assumptions, the goal is just a projected amount. The lower end of that range, in this case $50,000, should be the amount you'd be happy with (as opposed to ecstatic about).

One final way to calculate your request to the individual donor is to examine the person's past giving and ask for a certain percentage increase (usually 50 percent). If you are unsure, remember to ask for a range—between 35 percent and 50 percent, for instance. Organizations that neglect asking are frequently overlooked, meaning the gift goes elsewhere. Therefore, always ask, and ask for a specific amount, predetermined before the meeting with the donor.

WHAT ALL THE NUMBERS MEAN

Determining an individual's inclination and potential to give is both an art and a science. The science gives you a set of numbers; the art requires the fundraiser to understand how individuals use their wealth for charitable action and engages the values of prospective donors on behalf of an organization. (The technical work of prospect research is addressed in Chapter 5.) The "gift of significance" method helps ensure that trustees demonstrate the same level of commitment to your organization by giving according to their philanthropic potential. This tends to produce the best outcomes because it encourages the more affluent board members to make a greater personal financial commitment. At the same time, it doesn't alienate those members of more limited financial means from continuing to contribute to the board in other capacities. The mathematical determination of a trustee's potential to give is a good thing to be sure, but it's what one does with those numbers that engages the donor.

A HUMBLE AND REWARDING TASK

Before or even after you undertake your board tune-up, you'll likely run into some philosophical resistance from others who are skeptical of the importance of the CEO/board dynamic. Some people will say that boards come and go, while the executive is really the office that holds the institutional memory. Others will say just the opposite. But don't let either argument throw you. As it often does, the truth probably lies somewhere in the middle. A nonprofit organization is not owned by any one person or body; it is a public trust and, as a public organization, it's meant to be a good steward all around. You may find that in an age where the tendency is to overglorify individual prowess, the work of facilitating a group to achieve its highest potential can be a humble and rewarding task indeed.

———— ❧ CASEBOOK ❧ ————

At Caring Hospice, under executive director Aurelia, the board's hard-won proficiency as fundraisers runs parallel to the way they conduct their board meetings and operate as a team. A week before the meeting, a list of items for a "consent agenda" goes out. These are routine items and resolutions organized by the board chairperson and the CEO that don't need any discussion before a vote. Unless a board member feels that an item should be discussed further before a vote and requests the removal of that item ahead of time, the entire package is voted on at once without additional comment. This procedure saves a good deal of time. Previously, the board never had any time to discuss substantive issues. The consent agenda having been approved, board members are now free to focus on substance, such as long-range planning or strategic fundraising. The strategic impact of this step is just one sign of this organization's move toward a greater level of achievement.[11]

———— ❧ ❧ ————

AT THE END OF THE DAY

Higher-level fundraising requires an engaged board that knows its core strengths and knows where it needs to develop new strengths. Board members assure all aspects of their governance role and are not afraid of intentional conversations to evaluate their performance, including their own giving. A key aspect of the board is to make sure that the fundraising engine is working, which is different from assuming the board must be a leader in fundraising. To raise more money from your board, intentional conversations directed at gifts of significance are preferable to "Give and Get" policies.

CHAPTER FOUR

HIGHER-LEVEL THINKING FOR GREATER FUNDRAISING PERFORMANCE

IMAGINE, IF YOU WILL, THAT your nonprofit wants to deliver services in a new place or in a new way. Maybe you need to bring in new trustees or to revitalize your major donor program. Some of these tasks require analysis to identify problems, while others call for strategy. All of them are in need of higher-level thinking, an approach that requires not just distance but depth as well. Higher-level thinking takes your analysis and strategy and creates a methodology for you to achieve the change you are seeking. And it will raise more sustainable revenue for your agency compared with shallower, short-term approaches.

Let's explore this idea a bit further. Higher-level thinking assumes that in addition to strategic (three- to five-year) planning and long-range (five- to fifty-year) planning, an organization must continually search for previously undiscovered or new fundraising opportunities. The objective is to combat the existing mentality in which the primary duty of fundraising leaders is seen as simply funding their organization through the current budget year, as though tomorrow can wait. While I sympathize with this sentiment, it falls well short of what's possible, and ends up shortchanging organizations and their constituents. As we know, tomorrow will always be a mystery, but you can still use higher-level fundraising concepts today to prepare for the future and empower you throughout the years to come.

We saw in our discussion of organizational culture in Chapter 1 that raising significant revenue must occur in an organizational context, not a silo, and thus it follows that your organization's program design must also be integrated with the fundraising program. Long-term revenue, or "sustainable funding" in the parlance of the field, won't come about if fundraisers and/or the development program are isolated or downright ghettoized. Chapter 1 outlined several common organizational pitfalls that prevent an agency from securing its highest revenue goals.

Before moving to the second part of our book, which focuses on advanced fundraising tactics, let's take a deeper look at recurring "money" problems that are probably creating barriers to the growth and success of your nonprofit. In this chapter, I will ask you to reflect on the organizational infrastructure and day-to-day habits of your organization. Then I'll highlight and help you determine how to confront specific challenges that nonprofits usually face, which, when thought about at a higher level, can markedly improve your fundraising revenues. These issues are:

- Measuring and maximizing your organization's impact
- Creating a successful strategic plan by linking it to fundraising
- Determining your organization's appropriate revenue diversification
- Asking the necessary questions regarding your organization's sustainability
- Deciding your organization's position concerning collaborations and strategic partnerships
- Avoiding flatlining by confronting the brutal facts of your organization's reality
- Realizing your organization's biggest dreams through the right BHAG

A few years ago Dan Pallotta, the nonprofit innovator and author, called for an all-out paradigm shift in terms of development allocations. He wrote:

The sales spending yardstick for charities that deal with life and death issues should be human mortality rates, and nothing else. And until those rates are zero, the fundraising spent should correlate to whatever it's going to take to get to zero.... We have to start thinking about 50 percent to 100 percent fundraising rates for the organizations chartered to save human lives.[1]

At this writing, our sector is an order of magnitude away from heeding Pallotta's clarion call. Typically fundraising ratios wallow in the 5 percent to 15 percent range, buried within allocations to "overhead." While this situation may be great news for authors hawking books about the need for greater fundraising among nonprofits, it indicates a sad state of affairs for those who truly aim to change the world through their nonprofit organizations. I've seen the annual budget of a major nonprofit social service provider totaling $32 million whose allocation for fundraising was $79,000. That's barely two-tenths of one percent! Often in the audit process, a portion of the fundraising costs are (rightfully) allocated into the program expenses, which I understand and support. However, at an organization of this size with an annual budget of $32 million, only $79,000 for fundraising is dreadfully low. (Ironically, the organization complained that it couldn't understand why it wasn't getting support from major donors.)

Statistics like these cry out for some sort of higher-level thinking. But first, before we get started "thinking outside the box," let's at least get to know what that box really looks like.

THE IMPORTANCE OF MEASURING YOUR LONG-TERM IMPACT

A first step along the path to higher-level thinking begins with a look at impact data and its importance to your fundraising efforts. Why do donors give their money and other financial resources to nonprofits? What does your organization "sell" and of what value is it to the organization?

We all know the answers to these questions: Donors give because they are value aligned with the mission of your organization, and the fundraiser is in turn "selling" the impact of your services on the community that you are dedicated to serving. That's our product. There is no other.

Consequently, the measurable impact of your services is the holy grail for a fundraiser because documenting that impact allows the fundraiser to make the case for why a donor should support your work. If you don't know your organization's impact, or you can't substantiate it with data, then your case for donor support will be weak, at best. By extension, the longer the term of your data, the stronger the case you can make. A ten-year longitudinal impact study is more impressive than a one-year assessment. But even if you are a start-up, the data you use to justify your case doesn't necessarily need to be your own. You may be able to use "best practices" data or data from a recent study.[2] At the very least, be dedicated about tallying the number of people who use your services, any of the benefits they derive and what impact the services had.

In either case, your organization will eventually need strong evidence that documents the outcomes of your work and demonstrates impact. Otherwise you are liable to fall into the type of trap that befell a youth organization that I'll call Kids Forward (KF). KF had been in existence for thirty years, yet even though it could and did measure outcomes one year at a time, the organization was never able to say if its graduates actually saw their lives improved by having been in the program. How could such a vital and telling measurement go uncalculated, you may wonder. KF had no longitudinal (read: long-term) impact data because it had no vision of its importance. Or put another way, KF hadn't thought further and deeper. The need for deeper vision, which acknowledges and validates higher-level thinking, and the ways to implement it are our challenge as fundraisers.

Once you know your long-term impact data, the next step is to use the details of that impact to move to a higher level of service. "The way to maximize impact," says Dan Pallotta, "is not to fund a program that is having a great impact. The way to maximize impact is to fund a revenue engine that can multiply the dollars you are contributing."[3] In many cases, when translating impact into fundraising success, nonprofits may run up against the type of roadblocks outlined in Chapter 2, such as the taboo about asking for money or the systemwide prejudice about not funding capacity costs. Other nonprofits may see fundraising too narrowly, as a mechanical process, carelessly cobbled together with a minimal investment of time and resources and undeserving of any genuine strategic thinking. This, too, is misguided thinking.

For a nonprofit to succeed at ramping up services, purposeful and deliberative thought are required around all three fundraising poles: "the product" being sold, the targeted "buyer," and the "sales pitch" to close the deal. Successfully selling your organization requires a firm grasp of how your organization positively impacts your community blended with a clear picture of the type of donor you are hoping to attract. Too often fundraising leaders arm themselves with only one of these exigencies, which is the equivalent of bringing fifty cents to shop at a dollar store.

STRATEGIC PLANNING FOR SUCCESSFUL OUTCOMES

Enter the strategic plan. A focused strategic plan is the bedrock of a successful organization, as it establishes standards for evaluating program ideas to determine which ones fit the mission and which ones work against it. The strategic plan is broader than the fundraising plan, as it encompasses the whole of the organizational development: the impacts, the projected outcomes, and the plans over the long and short term. The fundraising plan (aka the development plan) is dependent upon the strategic plan. It is a subset, the same way that within the strategic plan you might have a communications plan, a quality assurance plan (for evaluation), a board development plan, and possibly a new trustee recruitment plan. There is an essential link between fundraising and strategic planning, though, and unfortunately, too many nonprofits overlook it, leaving the development/fundraising department to create its own decoupled plan. This is a poor course of action because it essentially blows up the bridge between programs and funding.

How you propose to fund your organizational future will inevitably influence your fundraising approach and ultimately determine your capacity to deliver whatever plans you make. An understanding of the Pyramid of Giving—Figure 4-1— is part and parcel of this decision.

Figure 4-1. The Pyramid of Giving.

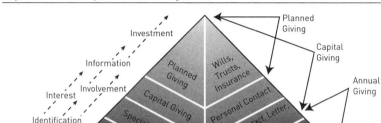

Donors ascend the pyramid as their commitment to the organization increases. In a sophisticated development operation, the goal is to qualify current donors at each stage and encourage upward movement wherever appropriate.

Annual Giving is the primary fundraising method used to broaden support, upgrade giving levels, and provide operating support for ongoing programs. Special/Major Giving, which I discuss in Chapter 5, comes from the top 20 percent or your donors. Capital Giving, discussed in Chapter 12, is an intensive, organized development effort to secure philanthropic gifts for specific capital needs or projects. Planned Giving, the subject of Chapter 13, is the integration of sound personal, financial, and estate planning concepts with the individual donor's plans for lifetime or testamentary giving.

The pyramid illustrates a fully functioning fundraising program, and how its various components build on each other. Too many nonprofits lack this deeper, comprehensive vision and mistake parts of the pyramid for the entirety of their fundraising engine. Remember development is an ongoing process, not an event.

When it comes to funding the future, a development professional's input is just as valuable as that of a program director. Therefore, even if your development director is not necessarily charged with altering the organization's mission, the director must nonetheless "sell" your vision for the future, especially if it is to come alive in the *donor's* real experience. A development professional can tell you if your plans for the future are realistic.

There's an old saying that goes, "Rich or poor, it's better to have money." While money is no guarantee of impact, it has the power to maximize it and ensure organizational stability. Here are important fundraising questions to consider when creating your development plan:

- How much does it cost your agency to raise a dollar?
- How will that cost rise over the next year or two?
- What revenue source or sources are likely to fund the proposed projects? Government grants, foundation funds, corporate giving, planned giving, or donations from individuals?
- Will you need to diversify your funding sources? If so, to what extent? And what is the lag time before a return can be expected?
- Will the cost of diversification be higher than the amount needed to run the new programs? For example, if your organization retains only a government grant writer, what will be the additional cost for an expanded staff or consultants? Should you consider outsourcing with a fundraising consultant instead of using in-house staff?
- Should you have more special events? Should the events be small parlor gatherings or large galas, or both?
- Will your funding last beyond one year, two years, and three years?
- Do you need a major campaign? If so, do you have enough individual donors to secure the lead gifts needed to start? If not, what steps should you take to get ready for a campaign in the future?

Relying on the belief that "if we build it they will come" is, in a word, unreliable. After all, *Field of Dreams* was just a movie. Reason suggests that you know what will be required of your fundraising program in order to plan for the future. For instance—and here again is where higher-level thinking is instructive—there is a qualitative difference between nonprofits and for-profits when it comes to "the bottom line."

For years, businesses had one bottom line; namely, profits. Sometime in the late 1970s, customer service and satisfaction was introduced as an additional bottom line. But a nonprofit has multiple bottom lines, made up of clients who benefit from the organization's mission, donors who require stewardship, all-volunteer board members who must be treated properly and proactively engaged, other types of funders beyond individual donors (e.g., institutions and governments), and especially the community at large. The strategic plan has to address pleasing these different constituencies, and the fundraising plan needs to be well thought out and aligned with the best revenue-producing strategy.

A dozen different development professionals might have a dozen different and unique fundraising plans, and each of them can be successful if their organizational strategic and fundraising plans are well aligned. Among other things, your fundraising plans should give guidance on the importance (or not) of funding diversification.

SHOULD WE DIVERSIFY, AND IF SO, HOW?

The conventional wisdom in nonprofits is that the diversification of funding sources is always a good thing and important because it provides nonprofits a safeguard against one funding source collapsing over another. The thinking is that a nonprofit should welcome the support of all comers: individuals, governments, foundations, and so on. While this familiar notion ("avoid putting all your eggs in one basket") makes a certain logical sense, higher-level thinking might call it into question. Let's examine what diversification is about, and then we can test how it stands up to your reality.

Diversification decisions usually need to change as an organization matures. In the early period of a nonprofit's life, the organization seeks revenue wherever it can find it in order to pay the bills. A broad diversity of funding sources seems sensible; the more the merrier, with room for everyone. The belief is that diversification acts as a hedge to risk. If one source of funding dries up, then other sources of funding will limit any damage from the loss. Still, the executive director of a nonprofit must ask, "Does this view of diversification really serve the more ambitious objectives and long(er)-term mission of my nonprofit? At what point does it hinder greater growth in exchange for more limited, near-term, and plodding operations?" The hidden fact is that sustaining too many revenue sources is laborious and costly.

Focus on Your Primary Funding Source

You might be shocked to discover, as I was, that size matters when it comes to diversification. Research on the merits of diversification shows that large nonprofits (those with annual revenues of more than $50 million) that were able to grow revenue concentrated their fundraising on one dominant funding source rather than on diverse sources.[4] Authors William Foster and Gail Fine actually argue against diversification, or rather against the conventional concept. As practiced by larger nonprofits, a focus on a single funding source neither decreased revenue nor increased the risk of lost revenue sources. So rather than diversifying sources, these organizations developed a strategy for diversification *within* a single funding source. In terms of higher-level thinking, they looked deeper instead of wider.

For smaller agencies, diversification has its place, though it comes with an attendant price. While it is important for some smaller agencies to have a backup in the event that one revenue source collapses, diversification is labor-intensive and often feels like trying to balance teacups on the end of a broomstick. Underfunding of diversification initiatives only exacerbates the problem. To do it well, diversification needs adequate funding and a multitude of talents on the part of the fundraiser or fundraising team.

For example, an organization that focuses on government as its primary source of funding might solicit funding from different levels of government; that is, federal, state, and local. The organization might also solicit different agencies within each level of government, and even multiple states and localities. Looking even more deeply, it might focus on soliciting funds from international governments and/or the United Nations. Unlike conventional diversification, this primary channel method, wherein one masters the nuances of the dominant funding source, reduces an organization's exposure to spreading itself too thinly.

Clearly, focusing on a single source of funding is most successful when an organization can readily identify which funding source is the most natural, lucrative, and accessible fit for the nonprofit's mission. The discipline required to identify that fit is usually an excellent sign of leadership, as well as the vitality of the organization's vision. As a nonprofit matures, it must carefully balance the passion of the first generation with the management skills of subsequent generations of leadership. Then, as time goes on, funding opportunities will rely less on the personal "subjective" qualities of individuals (e.g., charisma) and more on experienced management, which directs the organization toward the newer (and hopefully better) set of problems that go along with growth.

Additional Revenue Sources May Be Hiding in Plain Sight

Frequently, the best way to understand how to do something is to see someone else do it incorrectly. Take the case of Sisyphus, Inc., a popular summer camp serving about 3,000 kids. Of course, the name wasn't really Sisyphus, Inc., but that's how one board member referred to the organization because it emulated the mythical Sisyphus who pushed the rock up the hill only to have it topple back down each time he neared the summit. Sisyphus, Inc. had been around for well nigh fifty years. Each year the organization limped along until just before the end of the year, when the limp became a mad dash for last-minute funds to meet the annual budget.

When you looked at all the ways Sisyphus, Inc. could raise money, you'd see fees and grants in the foreground, but thanks to a lack of higher-level thinking, there was a potentially rich revenue stream hiding in plain sight that went completely ignored for half a century. Imagine, if you will, how many grateful parents there were of kids who'd gone successfully through the camp program, as well as satisfied "graduates" themselves. Yet the organization never developed a thoughtful approach to engaging these grateful parents and alumni after the program ended. Instead, Sisyphus invented a list of explanations for why it wasn't possible to fundraise through parents and alumni—a panoply of excuses based on speculation and fearfulness:

"They're not going to want to give."
"It's not our place to ask them for money."
"They should be able to see we need money without us asking."
"The alumni just graduated and don't have any money yet."

It was a thorough and thoroughly useless list. The last thing anyone at the organization had thought to do was to actually speak with the parents or alumni to gauge their interest in philanthropy. In other words, to think and act on a higher level. To remedy this situation, a "listening tour" was arranged in which parents and alumni were brought in to talk to the board. Those selected were the best and the brightest drawn from a series of focus groups that I, as their fundraising consultant, had conducted. When surveyed anonymously, the parents and alumni overwhelmingly expressed their puzzlement at never having been asked for money. The organization's revenue future had been right there all along, though it would likely have remained obscured were it not for the introduction of a new way of thinking.

So how does an emerging nonprofit determine the method of diversification appropriate to its present state of maturity? Overall, a good rule of thumb is to diversify your income slowly, with patient exploration, ensuring that you have the capacity to develop and sustain each of your revenue sources. You need to avoid taking on more development work than you can manage. Furthermore, some revenue sources may appear strong because of the skills and talents of the staff person or consultant who developed it, but they may not be the best fit for your agency. Here are two other important questions to ask:

1. *How much diversification do you need?* You can calculate how much diversification your agency needs by analyzing the past three years of budgets to see what shortfalls or surpluses you've had. Write down the numbers for each of those categories; then turn to each distinct area of your existing revenue and use the ROI calculator (see Chapter 2) to determine the efficacy of each one. Record your findings as the basis for an internal report. If you have additional time it might be wise to analyze your competitors' levels of diversification. You can find out their revenue stream by going to GuideStar.org and finding their Form 990, a public document that requires every nonprofit to list its largest revenue sources. In this way you can learn a lot about how diversified your peers are.

2. *How much risk should we take on?* To attract new revenue streams, you will have to develop and sustain new funding capacities because each requires, in essence, a separate approach. Each calls for specific skills, capital investment, and management expertise. Only then will each tactic be able to attract reliable operating revenue, pay the full cost of operations, and deliver a good return on your investment. Choose the revenue streams that work best for the skills and talents

of your team (or recruit the talent you need) and only stay with those revenue sources that return a good or high ROI. Remember, *lead time is required* before a positive return is realized, and until then that lead time must be continuously funded. For private grants, the lead time is usually eighteen months; for major donor cultivation, one to three years or more, depending on the size of the gift being pursued. Lead time for a campaign could be a year or so in the planning phase, four to six months for feasibility studies, and three to five years for the campaign itself.

Obviously, the objective is to recoup your investment once the revenue stream bubbles up, but if not, be careful not to judge your venture too soon. Just because your explorations didn't end positively doesn't mean your investment wasn't worthwhile. Hopefully you can learn why it failed and apply that knowledge to what may work in the future. Until you discover your most dominant source of revenue, and your most reliable secondary source, it's best to keep exploring the various revenue options available to you until you fully understand the potential of each one.

SUSTAINABILITY AND LONG-TERM THINKING

In recent years, the issue of sustainability has dominated the conversation between nonprofits and their funders. Questions concerning an organization's capacity to continue providing services to its clientele arise frequently on funder's requests for proposals (RFPs) and in discussions between nonprofits and donors. The questions are legitimate: Funders want assurances that a nonprofit has a future. Essentially they're saying: "We'd be interested in funding you, but what is your plan to wean yourself from us when we stop funding you, say, three years down the line?" As reasonable as these questions are, nonprofit leaders are still often at sea when trying to formulate an honest and accurate response. In fact, many nonprofits are so focused on near-term survival that they haven't had the luxury of considering the sustainability of their own programs and services.

Let me suggest a response to sustainability questions. But before I do, let's look into the question a bit more deeply. What does the funder truly wish to know? Consider this: Within the past five years, several icons of American for-profit business have stumbled badly and even disappeared. Remember Lehman Brothers and Bear Stearns? By that measure, is it fair for a nonprofit to have to demonstrate the long-term sustainability of its programs? I believe so, and I would urge you to reflect on how your organization can benefit from exploring sustainable revenue streams.

Remember, funders aren't asking for a strategy to provide revenue in perpetuity. They just want to hear that you have a real development plan in place.

At best, sustainability forecasts are limited to a finite and manageable period of time. Three years is about as far ahead as you can reasonably project for your annual budgets, five to ten years for your strategic goals, and twenty-five years for your long-range plans. So your answer ought to begin with a workable period of the forecast for your agency. It can be three years, or twenty-five years, as long as you are clear about the sustainability you're defining.

Your response should also infuse your candor with a touch of optimism. After all, sustainability is not just something concrete, like a building or an annuity. Rather, it is partly an aspiration, like "peace," "justice," or "prosperity." In the absence of a crystal ball, what you can demonstrate to a funder is that your organization has the capacity, the intent, and the heart to approach the objective of sustaining itself in the future (and that you don't rely on crystal balls as your determining methodology).

Here is a sample sustainability statement you can draw upon, borrowed from a community development organization whose annual budget is $2 million, but which leverages about $42 million to renovate or rehabilitate (mostly) abandoned housing:

Northern Commons Development Corps strives for sustainability in its fiscal heath as follows:

> *A key source of our sustainable revenue derives from development fees on our housing construction projects, whereby we secure 7 percent of the project's revenues. The difficulty with this revenue source is that it comes only after the projects are complete (eighteen-month project cycles are typical). Also, this revenue source*

requires NCDC to sustain an "optimal" level of new housing construction development, a pace that cannot always be maintained. These two facts often make cash flow in our base operations difficult. Once fees come in, we are more solvent, but just for the costs related to the developing project that includes staff and overhead.

Toward improving our cash flow, we [have] adopted a plan for the establishment and expansion of our individual donors. We are working with a professional fundraising counsel toward meeting that goal over the next three years. The plan calls for establishing a Board Development Committee and the purchasing of "value aligned" prospective donor lists to identify individuals of high net worth from our neighborhood who are value aligned toward our work.

THE INS AND OUTS OF COLLABORATION AND STRATEGIC PARTNERSHIPS

We can simply define collaboration as the process by which two or more organizations share knowledge and expertise to realize their objectives. Peter Drucker provided an even simpler definition at a conference I once attended. Said Drucker, "Partnerships are difficult. Period." In light of such a clear red flag, the ensuing question that arises almost feels Hamletian: to partner or not to partner? On the one hand, collaboration has great potential to benefit a nonprofit from the standpoints of organizational development, mission fulfillment, and fundraising. Greater access to financial support is especially important when competing for limited financial resources, and it can in turn produce greater service to the mission and quality recognition of the programs. But on the other hand ... what Drucker said: Partnerships are difficult.

Perhaps unsurprisingly, nonprofits as a group tend to have mixed feelings about the prospects of collaboration. For one, they are wary of joining with rival organizations. The leaders may also see the suggestion to work with other organizations to achieve their objectives as a criticism and may feel threatened by it. What's more, nonprofit leadership is frequently blind to the potential benefits and synergies that collaboration can produce.

But funders are cut from a different cloth when it comes to collaboration. Funders find collaborations especially appealing because strategic partnerships routinely create new programs and services. That reason alone beckons our sector to adopt, if not a fresh attitude toward collaboration, at least a fresh*er* one. You may recall the famous line spoken in Oliver Stone's film *Wall Street:* "Greed is good." A new take on collaboration for nonprofits might instead go something like this: "Greed *does* good." Foundation officers usually believe that collaboration is a means to amplify their philanthropic power. My view is that collaboration decisions must initially be driven by what's best for clients, and then if economies of scale provide better and expanded services, alliances should be discussed and realized, especially if it makes you more fundable.

Here, too, there is strength in numbers. Emerging nonprofits will likely have greater success in attracting funding and will make a more appealing case on behalf of any of their programs if they collaborate instead of acting as independent agents. When acting on their own as fundraising targets, many small and midsize organizations simply don't have compelling metrics to be considered by large funders, whereas when they work in concert with other agencies the opposite is true. Why? In part because collaborations help funders see their favorite programs connect with ever-larger groups of clients who benefit from these same programs. Greater light is also shed on programs that can be replicated and scaled so as to reach clients beyond the original target group.

You might then wonder, "Is my organization capable of contributing to and benefiting from a strategic alliance or partnership?" This question gets back to the issue of organization development. In my experience, organizations that have an outward-looking culture are inclined toward collaboration, and hence are more likely to reap its benefits. This is another incentive to reflect on your organizational culture and the opportunities it can create or prevent from occurring.

Let's look at two real collaboration scenarios to see how a strategic collaboration can garner the support of donors and create innovative programs. One scenario involved two organizations that provided social and health services to individuals living with HIV. Both organizations had successful track records supporting similar missions, but the first, Karetaker United (KU), was more active in designing outreach programs that attracted clients to its urban setting. The second group, Morrisbrook Community Services (MCS), was smaller and more focused on social services such as addiction counseling, and it operated in a suburban setting.

Neither KU nor MCS identified the collaborative opportunity themselves; it was suggested to them by a third party that had experience working with each of them separately. MCS offered valuable services, but it had a problem increasing the number of clients it served and was not sure how to move forward. Years before, KU experienced a similar issue, although over time it developed methods that markedly increased its success in attracting clients to KU social and health services. Therefore, the resulting collaboration consisted of Karetaker United training the staff of Morrisbrook Community Services in the development and practical application of community outreach. In terms of presenting the prospective program to funders, KU demonstrated its experience as an innovator that could replicate an effective program while MCS gained the expertise to establish a larger clientele and to attract more resources to support its mission.

A different strategic partnership involved Harlem Children's Zone (HCZ), under the leadership of Geoffrey Canada. Part of HCZ's mission was to improve neighborhood schools and the performance of their students, particularly through an initiative dubbed Truancy Prevention. One of the largest drags on overall school attendance in Harlem was a disproportionately high incidence of asthma among the predominately low-income student body. When HCZ learned that dust mites, roaches around the house, and a lack of adequate air-conditioning contributed to asthma, it began a collaboration with the department of pediatrics at nearby Harlem Hospital Center. With a boost from (augmented) funding from the Robin Hood Foundation, a comprehensive asthma screening and treatment program for the entire neighborhood was formed, known as the Harlem Children's Zone Asthma Initiative. In the words of the Initiative itself, "What distinguishes this effort from previous community-based health interventions in Harlem is that it was incorporated into an existing community-building initiative designed to improve children's education … provide families with safe and affordable housing … and improve residents' parenting skills…; thus, connections to needed technical, public, and legal services were facilitated."[5]

In each of these scenarios, the organizations pitched themselves as innovators developing pilot programs that could be replicated by other nonprofits with similar missions. The benefits of collaboration were also similar. Collaboration presents the opportunity to mature by helping you recognize weaknesses in your organization that create barriers to growth. Partnership teaches innovation. Thoughtful, effective collaboration creates the chance to transcend those limitations to reach the next level of organizational growth and success.

AVOIDING FLATLINING BY CONFRONTING THE BRUTAL FACTS OF YOUR REALITY

For all the higher-level thinking your organization will hopefully do, it must also be willing, simultaneously, to confront what Jim Collins calls "the brutal facts" of your reality. This is a critical concept as it relates to higher-level thinking because if you aren't honest with yourself, you can't ever hope to remedy your deficiencies, nor uncover the bold sparks necessary to transcend them. Just as we observed previously that most nonprofits wallow perpetually below the $250,000 annual budget threshold, many nonprofits also fall victim to a tendency known as flatlining. Flatlining in fundraising is when you exclusively rely on your renewals to sustain you, whether they are individual donors, foundations, or government contracts.

My experience is that roughly 40 percent of an individual donor base becomes antiquated every year. If you do the math, within about two and a half years, your individual donors will have all moved on. They'll often donate to the next hurricane or earthquake relief effort that comes along, which then leaves them less inclined and able to give to you. Some will have moved out of your area or died. Government contracts end, and foundations realign their priorities. Given this kind of turnover potential, living within your own spin becomes a form of organizational suicide. Our friends at Sisyphus, Inc. lived within their own thinking, but it had little basis in reality. Hearing the brutal facts of how their deficit was connected with their limited thinking was the only way to free them from their own closed orbit.

A former colleague of mine, the late Dr. Stephan Lentin, poetically referred to this self-examination process as "care-fronting."[6] It means you care enough to confront and bring up tough issues because you see it as an act of caring and compassion. You care enough to say how things could be different because you want them to be better. The key is to be as specific as possible, whether you are care-fronting a board member, an administrator, or anyone else connected to your agency. Care-fronting, alas, also requires care in its implementation. Rather than simply articulating problems, you can phrase your approach thoughtfully; for example: "We're better than this. It's not helping us to have X problem, and I need your help to try to solve it by the third quarter of next year." As with any critical analysis, the difficult facts of your agency exist along a continuum, colored in many shades of gray. For this reason, care-fronting is best used judiciously.

THE LARGE, HIRSUTE, AND BOLD WAY TO REACH THE STARS

It's been said that to achieve greatness you should aim for the stars and be willing to settle for the treetops. For any nonprofit director looking to truly change the world—and I presume that's what brought you into the nonprofit world—the star to aim at was first devised by Jim Collins and Jerry Porras[7] and it's called your BHAG (pronounced "bee-hag"). The first time I heard the term BHAG, at a Columbia University conference, I laughed out loud. It sounded like an old woman tending an apiary. It got even funnier when the speakers explained what the acronym BHAG actually stood for: *Big, Hairy, Audacious Goal*. Not exactly brimming with verbal decorum, to put it mildly. Yet the concept immediately resonated with me because I realized that the projects I had raised the most money for all had a BHAG: a big, hairy (i.e., kind of nutty), audacious goal.

I soon learned how common BHAGs were. One Michigan nonprofit's BHAG is to "Make Detroit a top-five city to live in by 2030." Another's big, hairy, audacious goal is to ensure that "More residents participate in Into the Streets National Service Day than watch the Super Bowl." BHAGs are so effective they have spread from the nonprofit world to the private sector as well. Microsoft's BHAG is: "A computer on every desk." Amazon's BHAG is: "Any book, in any language, in under sixty seconds."

BHAGs matter for many reasons, but for our purposes, the most important reason is that the bigger the idea, the more likely it is to attract larger funding. Small ideas get small money, big ideas get big money. Of course, sometimes big ideas and small ideas don't get any money at all, but if it's a good big idea and people are value aligned with it, they tend to support it because the big idea captures something that people want done in the world that they themselves can't do. This is one of the underlying reasons why people donate. They want to see something happen in the world that they themselves can't make happen—a sort of access by proxy to the causes that matter to them most as human beings. For instance, donors can't all go to Botswana and battle the AIDS epidemic. They are mostly thousands of miles away, worrying about their businesses, their kids, or their own part of the world. At the same time, they find it's unacceptable not to respond to the AIDS epidemic in Africa. So they donate to a reputable charity because they want to see someone address that problem. They are empowered through their beneficence.

How do you know if your BHAG is any good? The simplest test is when you first present it, listen for an audible gasp. Or a guffaw. Or a snide sort of chuckle. The level of audacity you're after is one that shakes people out of their normal comfort level and presents them with a whole new way of dreaming about their nonprofit. Back in 1961, President Kennedy's BHAG caused people to stop in their tracks and ask: "Did he just say he wants to put a man on the *moon*?" You too want your BHAG to be attainable, and only slightly insane (remember, NASA had already put men into orbit).

Paul Farmer, the head of Partners in Health, had a BHAG that worked brilliantly, though it initially caused gasping aplenty. Everyone else believed that eliminating drug-resistant tuberculosis in the barrios of the world was unrealistic because treatment was too expensive to bring to the poor. If you were upper-middle class, you could get sophisticated multi-drug-resistant therapies through your insurance company. But Farmer was in Peru, he was in Haiti, and he was in the gulags of the Soviet Union, and he thought, hairily and audaciously, "There's got to be a way to get this treatment to these people." He came up with a method and the UN funded his pilot projects, first in Peru, and then in the Soviet Union. George Soros, the great philanthropist, backed him and then Bill Gates backed him as well, and as a result Paul Farmer and his BHAG saved the lives of millions of people who would have otherwise died from drug-resistant TB.

If you're a small after-school program in a suburb of Cleveland, though, your BHAG can't be that "we want to change the way education is done throughout the country." That's not specific enough, and you're not the right people to do it. But you could have a BHAG of "creating an after-school activities program based on foreign language skills that is so revolutionary it will be adopted throughout Ohio, and possibly the entire country." A nonprofit called Health-Home Inc. has been working for five years on its BHAG, which is to reduce the spread of sexually transmitted diseases by 25 percent in an area covering 3 million people spread out over forty-five miles. The organization has successfully raised an additional $1.5 million toward that audacious goal from three funders who share the vision.

PUTTING IT ALL INTO PLACE

By now, I hope you're feeling ready to dig deeply into your organization's mindset with a fresh view of the role of fundraising in achieving your agency's mission. As mentioned in Chapter 2, the fundraising profession is a practitioner's profession, and thus no book about achieving the next level of fundraising would be complete without a trip through the myriad fundraising tactics that now await you. Whether you are at an embryonic stage in your organization's growth or already well advanced in your field, each of the tactics in Part Two of this book can be considered candidates for your consideration. You can think of them as arrows in your fundraising quiver. Read them in any order you like. May they guide you in your honorable quest to create a better world.

———— ≈ **CASEBOOK** ≈ ————

In the mid- to late 1980s, the great southern city of Richmond, Virginia, had an expanding homeless population because the old single room occupancy (SRO) hotels were closing. The three lead agencies responding to the homeless couldn't solve the problem on their own. One of the agencies was focused on mental-health services for the homeless; a second was focused on survival services; a third agency focused on group residences for homeless women. None of them were prepared to deal with the real estate and supportive service problems associated with losing SRO housing stock.

Making matters worse, the state legislature was extremely conservative on all the wrong issues, especially for those citizens without income. The lawmakers had never been asked to fund homeless assistance and, in fact, they'd never given any money to prevent homelessness or help its victims. This was the 1980s, and homelessness was a fairly new and frequently dismissed social crisis. But in spite of these clearly unfavorable political and fundraising conditions, a BHAG was developed to form two new organizations: one that focused on the legislature to obtain funding that would, in part, go to a second organization building new hotels for the homeless and mitigating the loss of the SROs. What made this BHAG even more hairy and audacious was that beyond the construction of new hotels, it called for appropriate support services so that the new buildings were healthy, healing environments, rather than unhelpful imitations of the run-down SROs that had previously defined the downtown corridor.

Thanks to this clearly articulated BHAG, the three main agencies were able to unify in their purpose, spending six months analyzing and diagnosing the problem and documenting how homelessness was increasing because of the disappearing SROs. They developed a plan to form the new nonprofits; they identified well-defined revenue streams and used the results from previously administered board surveys of the trustees from their existing organizations to see who would give a "stretch" gift to establish a new nonprofit.

The plan worked. Three years later, Richmond's Coalition for the Homeless and Supportive Housing Services had dramatically altered the makeup of housing stock in the downtown area and begun housing and servicing a homeless population that would have been otherwise condemned—literally—to a life of misery on the streets. By thinking at a higher level, these nonprofits achieved a mission they never before imagined was possible.

———— ≈ ≈ ————

AT THE END OF THE DAY

Higher-level thinking is essential to raising more revenue and preventing underfunding of the development program. In all instances, it will raise more revenue for your agency compared with shallower, short-term approaches. Linking your strategic plan and your development plan, analyzing what level of funding diversification is needed, knowing your return on investment, being proactive about partnerships, measuring and maximizing your organization's impact, and knowing your BHAG are essential to higher-level fundraising.

PART TWO

ADVANCED FUNDRAISING TACTICS TO RAISE MORE REVENUE

CHAPTER FIVE

BUILDING A DONOR CONSTITUENCY WHERE NONE EXISTS

INDIVIDUALS ARE THE LARGEST SOURCE of contributed income for nonprofit organizations. According to the Giving USA Foundation (www.givingusa.org), and as we see in Figure 5-1, total charitable giving in the United States reached more than $298.4 billion in 2011. Of that amount, fully 73 percent came from individuals. But finding new donors is perhaps the hardest fundraising task there is. It is process-oriented and time-consuming. Consequently, many fundraisers shy away from it, preferring to solicit stretch (i.e., larger) gifts from existing donors or ask those same donors to invite their friends, family, and coworkers to join them in giving. Frequently, though, the most difficult challenges can become the most lucrative. Building a donor constituency where none exists is no different, and as a fundraising tool, it bears considerable promise when done in a cost-effective manner and with a long-term view.

In this chapter we'll look at:

• How and where to uncover prospective donors
• The five steps to donor engagement

Figure 5-1. The giving pie.

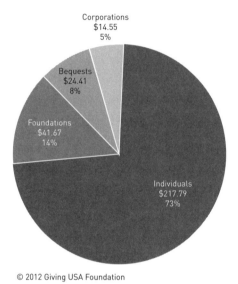

2011 contributions: $298.42 billion by source of contributions
(in billions of dollars – all figures are rounded)

Corporations
$14.55
5%

Bequests
$24.41
8%

Foundations
$41.67
14%

Individuals
$217.79
73%

© 2012 Giving USA Foundation

- The right kind of moves management (MM) program
- How to determine the right-sized donor constituency for your nonprofit

Let's begin by defining exactly—from a fundraising standpoint—what a donor is. As fundraisers, we don't consider a person who makes a onetime donation to charity to be a true donor. A true donor is someone who gives repeatedly and at increasing levels. (Chapter 12 examines the full evolution and trajectory of a donor over the long term; see especially Figure 12-1, the Pyramid of Giving.) True donors give over and over again because they are fired up about your mission. Building a constituency of donors is the process of identifying and cultivating prospects until they become true donors.

Successful donor fundraising is based on the marketing principle that a contribution is part of a satisfying mutual exchange that takes place between the donor and your organization. Your nonprofit facilitates that exchange by carefully analyzing the contributions marketplace and planning direct routes to the funding that seems ideal for your programs. Most of those routes run through board members, senior staff, advisers, and special friends of the organization. Their efforts are bolstered by clear, persuasive material that describes the needs of the group's constituents, the organization's work, its costs, and its projected results. When the exchange happens, your agency receives the funds and your donors get the satisfaction of knowing that they have helped to provide an important service or program.

HOW AND WHERE TO UNCOVER PROSPECTIVE DONORS

What seems most daunting about building a donor constituency is the idea that you are essentially starting from scratch. But looked at a bit differently, you may find that you are not always building from nothing; it just may appear that way. In science, there's a law known as the principle of mass/matter conservation, which holds that matter is neither created nor destroyed, it is merely transformed. A similar argument can be made about donors. Donors don't appear out of nowhere; they are constituents and potential constituents whose relationship to you is reshaped through your targeted outreach to them, your identification of their giving potential, and their interest in your mission.

In Chapter 4, I related the story of the summer camp whose graduates and parents were "hiding out in plain sight" as potential fundraising sources. The problem was that no one had ever bothered to ask them to contribute, which is one reason why it's wise for you to think less of "creating" donors out of thin air (in violation of the laws of physics) and instead imagine yourself helping to transform people who are not yet donors into those who will become them. Believe it or not, sometimes if you just solve the problem of collecting contact information you can be on your way to building your own bona fide donor database. In fact, contrary to what you may think, you don't even have to spend money to obtain the software required for a donor database. There are a number of free databases out there, such as Ebase, which is designed specifically for nonprofit fundraisers and can be readily downloaded (www.ebase.org).

Building a donor constituency where none exists essentially adopts community organizing and engagement methods in order to identify prospective donors who like what your program is doing to effect change in the world and want to become a part of it. A good and efficient way to tap into your community network is to start close to home by asking friends and coworkers who they know (including themselves) that might be interested in learning more about your nonprofit. Your goal is to identify donors who have the capacity to give and are value aligned with your mission. "Value aligned" is simply a fancy adjective meaning that they care enough about what you do to get involved.

Try to set up personal meetings with those prospects, or have them fill out an interest survey. Ask yourself, "Who else might care about what we do?" Whenever you find or are introduced to people who already give to other charities, or who are part of an affinity group sympathetic to your cause, attempt to arrange an interview with them to learn more about what causes interest them and why.

Beyond the general methods described so far, I'm going to give you a trade secret on how to uncover new value-aligned donors. Actually, this is less a secret and more an advanced methodology I've developed over the years that takes considerable time, but will consistently increase your donor pool when pursued with diligence.

The tactic begins with purchasing a mailing list of donor prospects who are likely to be value aligned with your mission. You can purchase such a list at any direct marketing mail house or online. There are "list brokers" in the field of direct marketing, such as Quality Letter Service, and you can shop your request to a few of them for the best price and the highest-quality list. List brokers will tell you what attributes the list has; for example, the names on the list all give to charity, they all live in the zip codes you serve, they all have incomes over $70,000, and they all subscribe to *Forbes*. Ask the list broker for as many details as the company can share.

The point of securing the list is not to mail to those on the list (not initially, at least). This is not a direct mail method. Instead, once you have secured the list, vet the individuals to learn more about their philanthropic interests and giving capacity. There is specific wealth-vetting software designed for this purpose. DonorSearch is one such prospect research tool providing information on donor giving history and assets. Check your nearest Foundation Center library for free access to this database.

Once the results are in from the vetting, issue a report and share it with your development staff and/or board development committee. Using the report, you can design personalized strategies to reach out to each of the individuals whom you identify as good prospects. Generally, I am able to secure 35 new prospects from every 100 people listed. Sometimes I call the prospects directly and invite them for a tour. Sometimes I choose to write to them, or I ask them to "friend" my agency on Facebook. It all depends on what the research reveals as their capacity to give. The higher their capacity, the more I want to reach them in a more personal way.

There is a direct expense associated with this process, usually around $0.45 per prospect, so for 5,000 initial prospects the cost will be $2,250. The larger the list, the lower the per-unit cost. I have vetted lists as large as 150,000 contacts. Ironically, many organizations already have a database of individual donors, but make the mistake of never deeply investigating the wealth potential of their constituents. Larger charities have realized the importance of having a strong donor giving program and investing the time to research their donors' capacity to give. Your agency will benefit by following suit.

Here are several other prospect-identifying activities you can engage in:

- Conduct donor prospect research on the individuals attending your annual events. The most promising prospects should also be considered for major gift cultivation and solicitation.
- Wealth-vet individuals who emerge from discussions with your board and staff to determine the best prospects for their cultivation. This should be an ongoing activity.
- Vet your potential nominees for a "Friends of" council (discussed in detail in Chapter 10). They may have access to philanthropy and/or a prospective donor network that could surface new prospective donors.

Virtually every cause has a target donor constituency, and those constituents are often already part of, and identifiable through, established affinity groups and networks such as LinkedIn, Facebook, Twitter, or other readily accessible social media.

LinkedIn presents excellent ways for identifying, qualifying, and engaging your prospects. At the very least, consider LinkedIn a tool that can provide a first look at a prospect's business information, career history, education, or professional interests. Some people also list their involvement in nonprofit and for-profit boards, their interests, and other achievements.

Facebook is another extraordinary resource for prospect information. You can use it to identify, qualify, and engage your prospects. Start by looking at your major gift prospects and their Facebook friends. Perhaps some of them are also alumni of your institution. They may have been friends or acquaintances while they were a student at your college, or even participants in one of your educational programs. Donors frequently stay in touch with colleagues via Facebook because they are on mutual nonprofit or for-profit boards. If you are a Facebook friend with such donors, you can ask them to make an introduction to some of their Facebook friends by suggesting you as a friend. They can create a post on their Wall asking their Friends to take a look at your organization's Facebook page or "Like" your organization. These are all potential ways to connect and possibly identify potential donors. Even those with whom you are not yet Facebook friends have pieces of information that they opt to share publicly, some of which you may find useful with initial qualification.

FIVE STEPS TO TRANSFORMING PROSPECTS INTO DONORS

Once you've begun to identify who you think might be interested in your organization, there are five steps to start transforming your prospects into true donors.

Step 1: Get to Know Your Prospect

Nonprofits need to build deep and sustainable relationships with their prospects. The first step of donor engagement is getting to know the prospective donors and letting them get to know you. This often takes the shape of a tour of your facility or a "non-ask" event, an introductory meeting set up by a friend of the organization. Some people refer to these kind of meetings as "friend-raisers." They are a chance for the prospect to hear about your mission, your work, and your successes. For example, many years ago a group of friends had a shared interest in making restitution to Native Americans for artifacts that formerly belonged to their tribes but had been given to museums instead. About twenty people gathered together based on this common interest to talk about possible approaches, concerns, and strategies, and to offer ideas for how best to organize. This is how their constituency-building process was begun. Today, that group is a national leader in its field.

Securing a new donor is achieved by giving the prospect an intimate experience of your mission. Like dating, charitable interest is based on passion. Your goal is to establish emotional connections. You can begin by inviting your prospects on a skillfully arranged tour of the agency, or to a well-scripted parlor event (discussed in Chapter 6), or you can even engage them through a stimulating virtual experience via the Internet.

At this point, some prospects will opt out of further engagement because they are not interested in your organization or because they are more interested in another organization and want to spend their time and resources there. Some people just won't be ready to commit to supporting a nonprofit.

For those who do show some interest, though, the next step is to …

Step 2: Get Your Prospect Involved

Your prospects have already gotten to know your charity. Now it's time for them to get involved. That might mean making a donation, but it's easier to get them involved at this step by asking either for their time (as volunteers) or for their advice and ideas. Most prospects will expect you to ask them for money, so you can pleasantly surprise them by instead asking for their advice on building a stronger organization, or for their help working the registration table at your next event. Remember, this is a *development* process, based on ever-deepening engagement.

While you can suggest ways for prospects to get involved, let them lead in deciding how they would like to get involved. My favorite question to ask at this point is, "How would you see yourself getting more involved with our work?" Some prospects will opt out of further engagement because they don't have the time or resources to help, or because they are just not interested.

For those who do get involved, the next step is to …

Step 3: Ask for a Small Gift of Financial Support

Now it's time to ask for a small gift of financial support. It can be an isolated gift or a contribution as part of an event, a fundraising campaign, or an annual appeal. Before you do, however, be sure you've followed up with your prospects several times over the course of a few months. If they offered you advice or an idea, have you taken it into consideration and/or implemented it? If not, do so and let them know before your next follow-up. I once called a prospect about a Youth Drop-In Center he'd toured and asked him what he thought. He said: "Can I be honest? The place is a dump. May I designate my gift to sprucing it up?" We agreed to designate half of his $25,000 gift to clean up and repair, with the other half going to program costs because, as we joked to each other, neither of us wanted a nice place with nothing going on inside.

For fundraising via text message, a small gift is $5. According to the Center on Philanthropy at Indiana University, the average annual household contribution to charity is $2,213, while the mean is $870.[1] These statistics can serve as yardsticks in determining how much to ask for, though a small gift is different for every donor and should ultimately be based on the individual's capacity to give. Once again, some prospects will opt out of further engagement because they don't want to make a financial gift to your organization or because they would rather give their money to other organizations (or, for a small subset, because they don't give to charity).

For those who do make a gift, the next step is to …

Step 4: Ask Them to Open Their Network of Contacts

Once your prospects make a gift, you'll want to keep them engaged as volunteers and advisers by staying in touch and continuing to answer any questions they have. This is also the time to ask them to help you by introducing your organization to more people who might be interested in supporting your cause. Ask donors to open up their personal network of contacts to help you find additional support. This process can take any number of paths. Donors can hold a small non-ask event to introduce you to their friends. They can send out a letter or e-mail on your behalf, or invite their friends, family, and/or colleagues to take a tour of your facility or perhaps attend your annual fundraising event. You might now want to ask particularly well-connected donors to join your board of directors or development committee.

Some prospects will opt out of further engagement because they want to support you, but don't want to get so involved as to introduce you to their contacts. Others will be uncomfortable with making such introductions.

For those who do make introductions, the next step is to …

Step 5 : Ask for a Major Gift

Once a prospect has gotten to know your organization, made a gift, and introduced you to his or her network of friends and colleagues, *and* if that person has significant enough personal (or business) wealth, now is the time to make a major "ask."

The ask might be a large multiyear annual gift, an endowment gift, or a contribution as part of a capital campaign. No matter the type of ask, by now you should know enough about the prospect to craft an ask that appeals to his or her own personal likes and dislikes, and you should have enough of a relationship to feel comfortable making this call.

I'm often asked how an organization decides what gift size constitutes a major gift. There is no single answer to that question because a "major donor" is a relative concept. It refers to donors whose contributions fall into the top 15 percent to 20 percent of your current individual donors, and the qualification in dollar terms will vary from one agency to the next. Also, what constitutes a major donor changes over the life span of an organization. A $25 million nonprofit that relies almost entirely on government funding might consider any individual who gives more than $200 to be a major donor. Conversely, a $2 million agency funded mostly by individual donors might define major gifts as those starting at $10,000. This is why I say it's a relative concept, based on factors other than overall budget.

You may find it effective to suggest a range to your donor. A word of caution: Beware of thinking, "So-and-so *should* give us X because they can afford it." You need to know your donors' circumstances and giving history. Just because they are wealthy doesn't guarantee they will give, or give generously. High net worth individuals are typically frugal, which means they are careful and meticulous about how they spend their money. This fact alone is sufficient reason to educate yourself about your donors at the same time that you educate your donors about your organization. The more your donors and constituents know about your nonprofit, the more justification they will have to support it. I believe there is a vastly underexplored swath of high net worth individuals who would be a natural fit as both donors and advisers to charities because so many of them share or have experienced the "entrepreneurial" atmosphere that is germane to all nonprofits; namely, lofty goals, tough challenges, high expectations, and limited resources. We are all more likely to support a cause that we feel mirrors our own experience.[2]

No matter how your agency defines major gifts, some prospects will opt out. Whether or not this is the case, you'll still need to continue the donor development process by cultivating these donors, seeking access to their networks, and keeping them informed of your fundraising and organizational activities. Most important, allow the prospective donors to decide for themselves if they want to be a part of your efforts. So many nonprofits prejudge their donors' interest and actually hold themselves back from pursuing possible candidates because they fear "it's not the right time" or "they already support the other agency, so they won't be interested in us." If that is indeed the case, your donor will let you know.

For most people, there are essentially three types of charities: those they really love, those they watch and support, and those they give to because their friends ask them to or because they live or work in proximity to the charity or its cause and they want to be supportive. A colleague of mine, Nick Lamont, who had never previously given to charity, gave $250,000 when his wife of twenty-five years succumbed to breast cancer. He was so moved by the hospice care she received that he made his first charitable gift to that program, in her honor. Giving for him was a tribute to his wife and a selfless statement that even those who cannot afford hospice care should have it. That's a value-aligned donor. The hospice continued to cultivate him in the years since the large gift and has enjoyed $25,000 in annual support. As of this writing, his total giving so far is $425,000. If the hospice had not had a thoughtful donor relations program in place, it would not have secured the initial gift or the renewals thereafter.

There is no doubt that Nick became a new donor because of the bittersweet experience of his wife's death; bitter because of the loss, and sweet because of the hospice's good care of her. But the skilled fundraiser also knew how to identify a prospect and research his potential to give, and he had the sensitivity to know when to ask for Nick's support. He uncovered a new donor because he had properly prepared to do so.

THE RIGHT KIND OF MOVES MANAGEMENT PROGRAM

At the start of this chapter, we defined a true donor as someone who gives more than once. When properly cultivated and engaged with a nonprofit cause, your donors should want to donate at increasing levels as they give. Over the course of their life, their engagement, passion, and commitment to your nonprofit's work is reflected in their increased giving and, ultimately, their planned gift from their estate. Moves management (MM) is the name for the tactics used by fundraisers to ask donors for more giving. At its most basic level, MM is saying to a donor: "You gave $200 last year. Could you possibly give $300 this year?" It's also known as "stretch giving."

But moves management is more complex than just "bumping up" your donors to higher levels of giving. It requires you to listen to and track your donors' interests so that you can suggest philanthropic opportunities and tax-efficient giving methods that match those interests. A solid customer or constituent relationship management (CRM) system is an essential part of streamlining and augmenting that process. You need to know what parts of your program your donors like best so that you can invite them to a greater contribution through increased giving, challenge giving, participating in an honorary council, and other similar donor engagement tactics. At the same time, CRM helps you maintain contact histories and supporter information for your entire constituency, be they donors, volunteers, partners, advocates, prospects, and/or board members.

Some people will be one or more of those things to your agency, and a CRM system will help you keep track of their status, as well as significant data such as whether your donor has a "pet project."

HOW TO KNOW WHEN YOUR DONOR CONSTITUENCY IS BIG ENOUGH

Oscar Wilde once remarked that "anyone who lives within their means suffers from a lack of imagination." In our nonprofit world, we don't lack for imagination as much as we lack a full understanding of how to fulfill it, which gives rise to this question: When is your donor constituency big *enough*? The short answer is that it's big enough when you've achieved all your fundraising goals. But in order to get to that point, and to avoid feeling like the proverbial hamster spinning perennially on the fundraising wheel, you'll need to know what your goal number is for success.

The first questions I always ask of an agency are, *How much money do you need?* and *Why do you need it?* These would seem to be the most basic of fundraising questions, and yet close to 80 percent of the people I ask are unable to give clear answers. Their vagueness and confusion exist because they haven't yet defined the steps they must take to go from where they are to the realization of their BHAG.

Although there's no one formula to determine the cost of these steps, once you've done your own math (based on your current status and BHAG), you will have simultaneously solved the problem of how big to make your donor constituency. Once again, the questions to pose are, "How much do you need?" and "What do you need it for?" That number should also include some cash reserves so that your organization is not living hand to mouth. Cash reserves generally run in size from the equivalent of three months to three years of your annual budget.

When most people talk about fundraising needs, they tend to mistakenly focus on year-to-year expenses alone. But facilities wear out, rents rise, and client needs and organizational goals expand and change over time. You may not know your "number" today, but you will need to calculate it in order to determine the size of both your minimum and optimum-sized donor base. Eventually you'll also have to verify your donors' interest and giving capacity, which we'll cover in greater depth when we discuss feasibility studies in Chapter 12 concerning major campaigns.

AT THE END OF THE DAY

Building a donor constituency where none exists is not an impossible mission. It requires an efficient process for locating and introducing prospective donors to a charitable institution they do not yet know. When done cost-effectively through personal introductions and careful research—including list purchases where the best prospects are researched and individual approaches are defined, the use of existing and free donor databases or wealth-vetting tools, and social networking (Internet-based and otherwise)—constituency building can yield not only a network of individual donors, but the fundraising expansion you most seek to reach your largest goals.

CHAPTER SIX

PLANNING AND STAGING COST-EFFECTIVE PARLOR GATHERINGS

FUNDRAISING PARLOR GATHERINGS GO BY many different monikers, including "ask" events or "parties with a purpose." Yet by any designation, these types of informal gatherings are far and away the most enjoyable fundraising tactic for fundraisers and prospective donors alike. They are an easy, inexpensive, relaxed, and efficient way to connect with potential donors and begin developing a relationship with them. What makes them so valuable is that they offer a cost-effective way to dramatically convey the impact your organization has on the lives of your clients, which is what Terry Axelrod, the founder of Benevon, has rightly called the "emotional hook" of your mission.

An informal fundraising gathering generally takes the form of an evening or weekend get-together at a donated space, usually someone's home, although it can also be held in private, nonresidential spaces such as an art gallery or studio. For obvious reasons having to do with human nature, events held in private homes feel less like "events" and more like friendly social gatherings. In the case of parlor gatherings, ambience matters because, as you'll see, you will be seeking to generate an emotional response to your cause from your guests, and there is something infinitely more intimate about gathering in someone's home.

In this chapter we'll examine:

- How to organize a parlor gathering
- The four key questions to answer at a parlor gathering
- Preparation and rehearsal of the gathering
- How to present your initiative to attendees
- A sample "run of the event"

Before we get into the nuts and bolts of organizing and successfully hosting a parlor gathering, let's take a quick look at some of the players and how an event generally unfolds.

SNAPSHOT OF A PARLOR GATHERING

The host of a parlor gathering is typically a well-connected person who may be a director of the agency, a major donor, or a volunteer. The guests are assembled largely from the host's personal and professional acquaintances. Modest refreshments are served. Guests are made to feel at home. In fact, the initial stages of the gathering feel like a party or reception.

Unlike a party, though, the gathering is tightly scripted. After a brief period of socializing, the host requests the guests' attention for a short program. The program is designed to be brief, informative, and above all, emotionally charged. At the end of the program, pledge cards are distributed and guests are invited to fill them out. Some are collected on the spot and others as the guests depart.

The event lasts approximately ninety minutes. People leave in good spirits, having made new contacts, had a drink, eaten some pastry or hors d'oeuvres, and most important, having learned more about an initiative that interests them. The fundraiser has not intruded on too much of their time. My experience over one five-year period was that the direct expenses were usually under $250, and the proceeds typically average $6,500, although depending on the cause and the guests, pledges can easily reach fourfold that amount, if not more. Since by now you are consistently calculating your return on investment, you'll see that even a modestly successful party in that capsule of time had an ROI of nearly 32–1.

Let's now examine the intricate parts and rhythms of a parlor gathering.

ORGANIZING YOUR GATHERING

The following steps to create and host your event don't have to be implemented in this precise order, though, as you'll see, there's a certain logic to the chronology of the tasks that is largely self-evident.

Identifying Your Party's Purpose

The first task in organizing any party with a purpose is deciding upon that purpose. The more specific the purpose, the more likely people are going to attend and ultimately give to your cause because donors always like to know exactly what their money is going toward. For instance, are you raising seed money for a new initiative? If so, how much? Whatever the purpose of your gathering, you and the members of your agency involved in running the party should be able to clearly articulate it in one simple sentence (e.g., "We are holding this event to raise $5,000 to purchase surveillance cameras for our new environmental protection site," or "We need to raise $18,000 to fund three scholars' participation in this year's International Forum for Child Welfare in Geneva").

Recruiting and Choosing a Host and Location

Once you've chosen your objective, you need to secure a host and a location for your gathering. The three most obvious hosting candidates are the organization's CEO, a major donor, or a celebrity (actor, politician, etc.) who is either practically associated with your agency or connected through affinity. These are the people most likely to draw attendees, to be passionate about your cause, and to own or have access to a residence large enough to host the event. However, these are merely guidelines. If you identify someone else who doesn't happen to match these exact criteria but who you feel best meets the needs of the fundraiser, then by all means go with your best available option. If you are still unable to find a willing host among these candidates or any of your other volunteers, you can consider asking for the donated use of a space, such as a studio, art gallery, or even the atrium or courtyard of a museum.

Your event location should be easy to reach for your invited guests, and well worth the journey upon arrival. Bear in mind when choosing where to host your gathering what might appeal to the donors you intend to attract. If your prospects enjoy the finer things of life, tasteful opulence is de rigueur. But if such trappings would call into question your agency's values, then a humbler venue may serve better. I have been to parties with a purpose held on antique trolleys, at a country barn square dance, and in the penthouse suite at the Ritz. No matter the venue, take a page out of any hospitality guide and do what you can to put your guests at ease.

Before you settle firmly on any venue, be sure to ask if there are an adequate number of restrooms, a place to hang coats (or to put a rented coat rack), a working audiovisual system if you need one, any artwork on the walls that might offend guests, a welcome area to sign in and pick up name tags, and so forth, just as you might if you were throwing a normal party that included acquaintances as well as close friends. An in-person visit in advance of selecting the venue is even better.

Sending Out Invitations

Once a host is identified and a date is set, it's time to prepare invitations. The host should be asked to provide a list of contacts for friends, colleagues, and business associates who might be interested in the agency and its programs. Board members, agency staff, and program volunteers may add their contacts to the guest list as well. Be sure to clearly indicate how to RSVP to the event so that you know how many guests to expect. There are several free online platforms, such as Evite, that can help you manage your guest responses, though some donors may prefer a paper invitation. Whatever you decide, remember to address the invitations to two people: either a husband and wife, or "you and a guest," which covers a person's friend or partner. This way, single people are encouraged to bring guests as well. Invitees are far more likely to attend if they are invited to bring someone they already know, especially if they think they might not know anyone else at the party.

To further ensure the success of the event, those people who compiled the lists should call the people on their lists and express the hope that they will attend. Even a voice message makes a big difference in ensuring high attendance. This step should not be optional.

Deciding on Speakers and Presenters

Who is the most effective speaker for your cause? Is it the most erudite, the most well-informed, or the longest-serving member of your organization? While any one of these people *can* be an effective speaker, these are not the characteristics that define effectiveness at a parlor gathering. So, while they should be taken into consideration, they should not tip the balance.

What you are looking for in speakers and presenters is this: Who is the most persuasive? Who can tell a great emotional story succinctly? Or, thinking counterintuitively, is there perhaps someone poorly spoken but whose every word an audience would hang on? These are the qualities that will persuade your guests to donate. Emotion, particularly empathy from your guests, will always carry the evening. The most effective gatherings are those where people directly served by the program are on hand to give personal testimonials.

Pitching Your Initiative

Remember that even though you are organizing an informal gathering, you are there to put on a show; therefore, many of the rules of show business and storytelling apply here, too. When you "pitch" your initiative, you only have a few minutes to convey information and to generate emotion. You may feel as if you are asking for a great deal of money and need time to explain why, but these two factors don't correlate in the context of a parlor gathering. In fact, long-windedness typically diminishes emotion and may cause you to lose your guests' attention. Consider this: Every day in Hollywood, multimillion-dollar movie ideas are pitched to financiers in three minutes or less. Clearly with stakes that high, they must be on to something.

Brevity isn't only the soul of wit; it turns out it's the order of the day when it comes to selling an idea or initiative. If your donors are anything like most wealthy individuals, their days are filled with people pitching them ideas or initiatives, and their expectations about what constitutes a good pitch don't change just because business hours are over. The speakers you choose must be able to articulate a brief, clear, simple message and create a personal, emotional link to the initiative they pitch—for example, "We need these cameras to prevent Polluticon from contaminating our freshwater supply and poisoning children and their families."

THE FOUR KEY QUESTIONS TO ANSWER AT A PARLOR GATHERING

No matter what you are raising money for at your gathering, there are four unspoken questions that can be the key to how much money you raise. Your speaker must be able to answer convincingly:

1. Why this initiative?
2. Why now?
3. Why are you the right people or organization to carry it out?
4. What will the donor receive in return?

This last point is especially salient. As with any donation, you want your donors to feel that they've given their charity in return for something of value. This simply means that your pitch needs to include a sentence or phrase of acknowledgment along these lines: "Thanks to you, the world will soon be different."

One final note on speakers: A sense of humor is another helpful trait to seek in choosing your speakers. Humor sets an audience at ease and can often open an emotional gateway to empathy. You want your guests to have a good time as well as feel as if they are contributing to a valid cause. One of the greatest nonprofit fundraisers of all time, Jerry Lewis, was a master at combining humor and empathy during the many years that he hosted telethons for the Muscular Dystrophy Association. In a sense, you can think of your parlor gathering as a microcosm of that large-scale televised event.

PREPARING FOR YOUR PRESENTATION

Now that you have your purpose defined and your host, message, and venue in place, there are a few steps remaining that will elevate your gathering to a truly higher level of excellence and intimacy. These simple tasks can and often do make all the difference.

It Pays to Rehearse

Sometime before your actual event, even just an hour or so before it begins, you should gather your participants and run through the presentation portion of the evening. Pretend it's the actual event and maintain "performance conditions." Is the audio/video cued up and working? Who is going to stand up when, and with whom? Time your speeches. Are they really as short as you think they are? Is anyone else covering the same material? Eye contact with an audience is so much more effective than reading from a piece of paper, but making eye contact may take practice. Even if your speakers don't feel they can speak "off the page," they will at least exude greater confidence in the convictions they discuss if they've had a chance to rehearse.

Selecting Your Presentation Materials

Would your presentation be more effective with audiovisual materials? What about other material exhibits of the matter at hand, such as a copy of the lease for a formerly homeless person you've helped to find housing? What about a signed letter of support from the Environmental Protection Agency? At a parlor gathering it's important to remember that you are not conducting a lecture; you are seeking to connect your guests to your initiative in a way that will make them want to act. A well-prepared handout that your guests can take home with them after the party will free you and your speakers from having to cram a host of information into a short amount of time, and it will ensure that what you do present will be reiterated later on, with the correct contact information for those who want to act or contribute further.

ON WITH THE SHOW

The gathering is upon you. The hors d'oeuvres have been served, the guests are all seated, and it's time for you to powerfully express the reason for the evening's gathering. The host and executive director make brief welcoming speeches. Here are some ground rules to observe:

- No speaker holds the floor for more than five minutes. Three minutes is ideal, but five should be the absolute maximum.
- After the wrap-up, guests should be invited to mingle or ask questions of the host or executive director.
- Informational packets should be distributed as the guests depart.

Here's a sample "run of events" you can use as a guide for your next parlor gathering. Feel free to adjust it as best suits your event.

Event Timeline

- Hors d'oeuvres and drinks: 30 minutes. Alcohol is at the discretion of the host, as agreed to in advance. Guests should be greeted at the door. Agency staff performs sign-in functions and distributes name tags.
- Welcome speech by the host/hostess: 2–5 minutes. The host should make three speaking points at most.
- Welcome speech by the executive director of the agency: 2–5 minutes. The focus should be the organization's history and mission.
- Testimonials by program clients and/or volunteers: 5 minutes (maximum).
- Inspirational talk on "How You Can Be Involved": 5 minutes (maximum).
- Host's thank-you to the guests for coming to the event: 5 minutes. The host also announces that the program director or executive director will be available to personally answer questions throughout the evening. The host invites people to stay for more refreshments and chat.
- Wrap-up: 30 minutes. Pledge cards are distributed throughout the crowd and collected as guests exit. Informational packets are distributed to departing guests.

After the party, one of the most often-heard complaints from donors and your event volunteers is, "No one even said 'thank you.'" Make sure your organization takes the time to send thank-you notes to everyone involved, including volunteers, staff members, and vendors. Keep your donors happy. You are probably going to be asking them for another donation somewhere down the road.

CASEBOOK

The first time I ever threw a party with a purpose, we served donated breakfast and raised $75,000. I was delighted and amazed. Then, as if that opening salvo wasn't enough, one of the attendees offered to host a second gathering the very next week and we raised an additional $110,000. My amazement morphed into utter disbelief. In only two events we had successfully raised $185,000 of our $250,000 goal. Sure, the party was for an excellent cause—the opening of a new seventeen-bed residence as a transitional program for adolescents in need. But the real keys to our success were our two cohosts, a husband and wife team that everyone knew and held in extremely high regard. Not only did they avail themselves of a profusion of excellent contacts whom they invited to the gatherings, but they themselves were able to advocate movingly on behalf of our cause. They knew their audience and how to reach them. In fact, they in turn were so moved by their friends' generosity that they donated the balance of the funds needed, and our renovation drive ended.

I wish I could tell you that every parlor gathering I've been a part of since had similar or better results than that initial home run. But alas, I can't. Still, that first experience speaks to how valuable the right hosts can be, and how infectious the act of giving can become at a well-hosted parlor gathering. Of the forty total attendees we had at the two gatherings, thirty-eight of them became new donors to our organization (the husband and wife were already donors). So not only did we raise money, we expanded our donor constituency and had thirty-eight new networks to explore for future giving.

Not all gatherings will be lucrative in terms of dollars, though all of them should be effective at identifying new potential donors. However, this is not to say that all parlor gatherings should go forward. On the contrary, if you can't arrange the necessary criteria—the right hosts, the right purpose, the right venue, the right kind and number of attendees—you'll be well advised to cancel the planning process and start fresh another day, rather than proceed with insufficient resources and momentum.

AT THE END OF THE DAY

Parlor gatherings are an enjoyable and cost-effective way to raise money and engage new donors. Though structured like parties, they are tightly scripted, condensed events that thrive on emotion and show your organization at its most impactful. Make sure you've rehearsed the "emotional hook" and have chosen a warm venue and persuasive speaker.

CHAPTER SEVEN

CHALLENGE GIFT DRIVES AND CORPORATE MATCHING GIFTS

ANYONE WHO'S EVER LISTENED TO a public radio station in this country will be familiar with the concept of a challenge gift drive. Deep into the annual pledge drive, the radio host announces something like: "Sponsor X is committing $5,000 toward our goal of $10,000, but only if we can raise the rest of our goal by the end of the month," or "Sponsor Y will match, on a 1:1 basis, each of the first $5,000 in gifts we receive until the end of the month." No matter what your taste in radio programming, these time-sensitive pledge drives are inevitably irritating to listen to (even professional fundraisers would rather hear music). Yet they continue to endure. Why?

Before I answer that question, think for a moment about how many times in your daily life as a consumer you've heard the expression, "Our sale ends tomorrow." Have you ever noticed that, though you may not have the slightest interest in what's being sold, a little voice in your head can't help but contemplate buying something before that sale ends? Such is the power of what fundraisers and salespeople alike refer to as a "ticking clock." Your brain may not even register what's being sold; what registers is that the sale *ends* tomorrow, just as our radio host in the previous example reminds listeners that "your donations will only be matched for another thirty minutes."

The notion of the ticking clock is a recurrent theme in our journey through higher-level fundraising. In Chapter 8, we'll take a look at the holy grail of ticking clocks for fundraisers—the last four days of the year. But before we go any further, let's quickly return to our fundraisers at the public radio station. During those "urgent" thirty minutes of the challenge, anyone who's ever thought about giving, or who has pledged money in the past, is almost forced to think, "If I give now, it'll be like giving double or triple the amount. If I wait past the deadline, my gift will only be worth half or a third of what it could be."

Is it not easy to see how these drives can potentially accelerate your nonprofit's fundraising?

The approach works because it is tied to a sense of urgency. The ticking clock trumps all, if you will. In fact, oftentimes a donor will still give a challenge gift even if other donors failed to live up to the challenge. Because they can jump-start a campaign, or act as a midcourse correction to energize a flagging campaign, challenge drives are almost always an integral part of capital and endowment campaigns. They are equally effective in annual fundraising, sponsorship, and any other effort to secure underwriting, all for a negligible increase in your overall fundraising costs.

A similar matched-giving alternative for nonprofits exists within the realm of corporate matching gifts. Corporations need tax writeoffs as well as opportunities to burnish their public image through good "corporate citizenship." One of the ways they accomplish these two objectives is by matching their employees' charitable contributions. As with challenge giving, the matching ratio some company programs offer for each dollar donated can reach as high as 4:1. Yet surprisingly, this rich potential resource goes largely underused.

In this chapter, we'll examine:
- How to put together and carry out your challenge gift drive
- Best practices in challenge giving
- Challenge giving and your board
- Corporate matching gifts and how to increase them

Perhaps nothing in this entire book speaks more directly to the idea of generating revenue to get your organization to the next level than the tactics we are about to delve into. Each is a way of turbo-charging donations so that contributions are received exponentially.

HOW TO PUT TOGETHER YOUR CHALLENGE GIFT DRIVE

A challenge gift drive begins when a donor makes a substantial donation. Usually it's a trustee or someone who knows and trusts your organization and has been giving for a while. Someone in your fundraising department realizes that now is a terrific opportunity to encourage giving by others. The fundraiser chats with the donor, and then if they are in agreement, you launch a challenge or gift drive, following the guidelines that you and the donor work out and sign off on. Guidelines can include whom to target for the challenge, when the donor pays (up front or when the challenge is met), and how the challenge will be advertised or marketed.

In some cases, donors will propose a challenge gift on their own. However, if your strategy is to wait until that happens, be forewarned: You are more likely to grow old than grow rich. The urgency behind challenge giving needs to begin with you, the fundraiser. Develop a proposal and take it to a major donor. Spell out what the challenge gift will do to help raise more money from other donors. A challenge gift is focused on a specific issue to solve a precise problem. It's not a general appeal; rather, it's a targeted effort to solve a problem that's easy to understand and articulate. You can and ought to show the major donor how much a challenge boosts response compared to a typical appeal. Use the same pitch on the board. It's all about leveraging the money.

If you don't know what it will cost to complete the project at the heart of your challenge, take the time to figure it out. Just because you or the challenge donor thinks "x amount" of thousands of dollars will be sufficient doesn't mean it will be. Another question to consider is timing. Given that a challenge drive can increase giving by 30 percent, do you use it to pump up donations in a slower part of the year, or do you capitalize on your best giving season, say, end of year? Most signs point to the latter option as your best one, although it's up to you to do what best suits your agency's fundraising needs.

THE THREE KEY STEPS TO CARRYING OUT YOUR CHALLENGE GIFT DRIVE

Implementation of your drive involves finding the right individuals to take the lead, coming to agreement about procedure, and getting the word out. Those three steps should unfold as follows:

1. *Make a short list of those donors you can ask to make a challenge gift.* In the absence of a challenge donor, I recommend you identify several possible donors and assemble them in order of priority. The prospects on your list should include the most thoughtful and current donors—the ones who truly "get you" and what you do. Focus on top prospects, and solicit lead donors in person. Many fundraisers start with the board chairperson, then move to the development committee chair, then to all the trustees, then to donors who have given significant gifts before (aka lead givers), and then to the community at large. As with any major gift fundraising, if a prospect replies, "I'll think about it," be sure to ask, "When is a good time to get back to you?"

2. *Write an agreement or pledge, once the challenge gift is secured, that explains the terms binding the donor's promise, even though it's unlikely that it would be truly legally binding.* Donors can, and at times do, withdraw and cancel their pledges for various reasons, although in my experience it rarely occurs. Nonprofits hardly ever take legal action against them. But memorializing a pledge in writing will inevitably reduce the chances of misunderstandings and hurt feelings. Keep your agreement simple and avoid a lot of "legalese." Here are some basic points to cover:

    *   How much will the donor give in total? This amount can be stated as: "$_____ if no funds are received for the challenge and up to $_____ if the challenge is fully met."
    *   Does all giving count toward meeting the challenge, or only new donations from first-time donors and increased donations from previous donors?
    *   What is the time frame within which the remaining funds are to be raised? (Thirty to ninety days is customary.)
    *   Will pledges count, or must the challenge be met with cash in hand?

- Can the match apply to granting foundations and corporations as well as individuals? What about net proceeds from a special fundraising event?
- Will the donor allow the challenge to be publicized and promoted, and agree to be named as the challenger? This request may require some finessing, though it is well worth trying as it lends a "human" touch to the challenge campaign. You can even name it: "The [insert donor's name] Challenge"—unless, of course, the gift comes from an anonymous donor. In that case, an artful name focused on your drive's goal can be set, such as "The New Playground Challenge" or "The Stop the Violence Challenge."
- What is the match ratio? Will it be 1:1? 2:1? 1:2?
- What happens if you don't meet the entire challenge? In the best case you can get your challenge donors to still give their gift, but remember that they are certainly under no obligation to do so. I recommend you ask up front.

3. *Promote the challenge and its progress in your newsletter, on your website, by e-mail, and in your local community newspapers.* Leverage the free coverage you can get from a journalist doing a story about why you have the challenge drive. When you pitch the story to local editors, focus on what the drive seeks to accomplish, not the drive itself.

A challenge gift may help you secure new donors or renew lapsed donors. Most evidence points to the success of challenges in stimulating response among active, current donors. A challenge gift not only increases giving levels of current donors, it elevates their thinking about what level they could be giving in the future. It also reinforces and tangibly demonstrates the concept that "the sum of our giving is greater than each individual's part."

BEST PRACTICES IN CHALLENGE GIFT DRIVES

There have been cases where those who gave under a challenge drive later reduced their subsequent contributions, resulting in a net reduction of total contributions to the agency's overall giving efforts. Some call this effect "donor fatigue," though I'm not a fan of that term because people are too complex for such easy categorization. Thus, in addressing this issue—by any name—it's important for you to be proactive and let your donors know up front that maintaining their regular support is essential. Let them know, "We don't want to fix one problem (meeting the challenge) by creating another (losing your funding for our regular, ongoing work)."

A fundraiser I spoke with about this problem told me that one of her donors concluded that, with the advent of large challenge gifts, his small gift would no longer be needed. She became worried that others might get the same impression, so she quickly issued a donor survey to gauge how her other donors were thinking. Thankfully she learned that only one other donor had a similar attitude about small gifts. The lesson here is that it pays to verify attitudes within your donor base rather than assume them.

Here are some other best practices to apply to your challenge drives:

- *Big goals get big gifts.* Increasing the target fundraising goal in a challenge drive has a significant effect on the size of the average gift.

- *Customize an appeal letter and the amounts you request.* Although customization of donor appeals is time-consuming and possibly costly in the short run, there are clear rewards to understanding the mindset of each donor in order to send the most personal and effective appeal. Customization can usually be done through a mail-merge process. While it's not necessary to create a different letter for each individual, you may want to do so for your top givers.

- *Offer money-back guarantees.* In your drive, state that if the minimum challenge is not met by a certain date, your donors' contributions will be returned to them. Your appeal could read: "By May 1, we must raise an additional $10,000 to match the donor's $10,000 challenge; if we fail to raise that full amount from you, our supporters, we will not be able to open the new environmental justice program for our teens, but we will refund your donation promptly. Please help us achieve our goal."

- *Create an air of exclusivity.* Let the donor know how many people you are approaching: "You're one of thirty-five people we're personally approaching for support." Donors often think that you have thousands and thousands of others to turn to. It's important that you define the context of their engagement in real numbers. It conveys the importance of their unique participation.

- *Create mailers your donors will open.* If you are using the mail, the battle is often getting the recipient to open the envelope. Consider posing a question on the bottom left of the envelope exterior, such as: "Do you know what our kids want the most?" Or use a sentence-handle such as: "The most important thing we can do right now to preserve our environment is …" I often suggest using large colorful envelopes that draw attention to themselves in the mail stack, or eliminating the envelope altogether and using a large postcard, or folding the mailing in half and wafer-sealing it. Be sure to check with the post office first so that your design meets postal regulations. I also recommend using fonts like Courier New 12 point, which is easy to read, clean, and looks very personal. Mail your challenge gift requests two or three times—at the start of the drive, midway through, and near the end—and be sure each time not to mail to those who've already responded. Too many nonprofits only mail once—a common and avoidable mistake.

- *Learn about your area.* Fundraisers have found that the location of a drive often affects its efficacy. Some areas are simply better than others. If you are going to try the challenge strategy for the first time, do some due diligence and seek out the experiences of others in the area, or your local chapter of the Association of Fundraising Professionals.

CHALLENGE GIVING AND YOUR BOARD

One ancillary but significant benefit of challenge drives is their potential effect on your board. The challenge process can inspire your board to revitalize its development committee, which is a subgroup of the board that encourages peers to fundraise and make personal contributions. The development committee chair should discuss the board's fundraising, giving, and progress toward meeting the challenge at every board meeting.

The challenge period is also an opportunity to include explicit language in the board members' job description about fundraising and giving. You can even utilize the challenge to engage board members in your annual fundraising events as host committee members and event planners. Your development staff should be working closely with the board at this time to expand your current donor base through prospect identification and cultivation of new and lapsed individual donors.

CORPORATE MATCHING GIFT PROGRAMS

As I mentioned previously, there is another important type of matching gift that happens outside of a challenge drive. Corporate matching, as it is known, was begun back in 1954 by General Electric Company. Through its Corporate Alumni Program, the GE Foundation began making matching gifts to colleges and universities, eventually expanding to other areas of charitable giving.[1] Today, countless companies such as Johnson & Johnson, Microsoft, and Union Pacific Railroad match employee contributions, sometimes at a ratio as high as 4:1. Naturally, some companies have overall and/or per-employee limits to their matching programs, but the leveraging power of these programs is nonetheless formidable. A 2012 survey by the Committee Encouraging Corporate Philanthropy found that 83 percent of surveyed companies offered at least one matching gift program.[2]

Though some agencies, such as political organizations, sports teams, and religious organizations, are restricted from applying for corporate matching programs, your own agency is quite likely eligible. If your church, synagogue, mosque, or meetinghouse focuses on community outreach, you probably qualify as well.

Increasing your fundraising through corporate matching doesn't cost more, though it takes some extra dedication from your fundraising team. To begin with, most individuals outside of the nonprofit sector have never heard of, and have never used, employee matching gift programs, so you'll have a lot of promotion and explaining to do. You may also worry about how to manage this work owing to staff or volunteer time constraints. Worse, if yours is like most development efforts, you probably have very little information on where your donors or their spouses work, and even when you have that information, you must still keep track of employee-giving programs at all of the companies where your donors or members work.

Finally, assuming you can manage those areas of focus, there's still the challenge of letting your donors know the appropriate process, guidelines, and steps so that they can complete the matching gift requests on their own. Is it any wonder that much of the available money goes untapped?

Thankfully, there are tactics in your fundraiser's toolbox that will help you ford this procedural and bureaucratic stream. If you lack sufficient staff, you can ask a volunteer to study and learn about this unique area of giving. Another option is to use a free searchable web page on corporate matching, such as those offered on the websites of most major universities (Stanford, Penn, American University, for instance). These services allow donors to instantly determine their eligibility and access company-specific program requirements and forms. You can provide donors with a list of corporations that offer these programs (also available for free online at http://www.doublethedonation.com/mowsf.php and many other sites) and ask them to check with their own employer.

As you begin unearthing corporate matches, try to walk in the shoes of your donors and think through all the ways they might get stuck in getting their employer's match. Address their issues in advance. Make it easy for them and guide their charitable actions. Instead of simply asking them to check with HR on corporate matching programs, provide them with the necessary guidelines and forms.

Whether you help your donors find a corporate match or take the time to organize and implement a challenge drive, your potential benefits will easily outweigh the costs of your extra fundraising efforts. Your impetus is clear: By going the extra mile, you could be receiving double, triple, or even quadruple the donations you might obtain otherwise.

─── ≈ **CASEBOOK** ≈ ───

Brian Feller sat across from me at the local café, distraught over the recent death of his adolescent son Kevin, who had succumbed to a rare blood cancer. He had been crying so much he had no more tears left, just sunken eyes. My heart went out to him. Brian had seen our nonprofit's flyer calling for volunteers at the local Krispy Kreme doughnut shop and decided to respond.

"Kevin was moved by the work you do with helping poor people get a home," the father said. "He saw you on the news. And then, when I saw this flyer, I knew he'd want me to reach out."

Brian told me all about his love for his son. I listened and wished I could raise the dead. Brian said he wanted to help, so I told him about our volunteer opportunities, but that didn't satisfy him. He wanted to help in a big monetary way. So I asked him where he worked. "Philip Morris USA," he said. I knew their giving programs well. They had a multitier matching gift program.

Brian wanted to donate $25,000 in honor of Kevin. "Let's both do some research and get together this time next week," I suggested. When we reconvened the following week, we were able to determine that the company would match his gift three to one! Brian's $25,000 generated an additional $75,000 from his employer, for a total of $100,000. Needless to say, it made his tribute all the more meaningful.

———————— ❧ ❧ ————————

AT THE END OF THE DAY

Challenge gift drives can unlock exponential giving, often doubling, tripling, or quadrupling the size of donations. The same is true of corporate matching gifts. Because challenge gift drives thrive on a sense of urgency, doing all you can to learn about and assist your donors will go a long way toward crafting the right kind of drive, or the right corporate match for your agency. The easier you make it for your givers, the more likely they are to contribute.

CHAPTER EIGHT

REAPING THE BOUNTY OF YEAR-END GIVING

THE GENTLEMAN BANK ROBBER WILLIE SUTTON was famous for saying that he preyed on financial institutions because "that's where the money is." In Sutton's line of work, the *where* question was the fundamental one. Had he been a more conventional fundraiser, he might also have considered the *when* question: "When is the money there?"

From the fundraiser's standpoint, a harmonious convergence arises at the end of every year between two emotionally disparate elements: warm holiday cheer and cold income tax necessity. One of every three dollars donated to nonprofits is transacted in the month of December alone.[1] Some wealthy individuals wait to see which stocks they should donate to get the best tax savings, while self-employed individuals whose monthly income varies often wait until year's end to get a clear sense of their financial picture and what's left for charitable contributions.

It becomes incumbent upon every nonprofit CEO to learn to master the finer points of the holiday season. In theory, the Year-End Drive (YED) is the culmination of your direct mail program. Hopefully you've been in contact with your donors several times in advance of this final effort. The industry standard is eight interactions with your donors per year, with a combination of phone calls, letters, newsletters, e-mails, and, ideally, in-person tours at your program site. The combination of other social service agencies looking for year-end gifts and the frenzy of holiday shopping makes this a very competitive time of year to get your donors' attention. This chapter takes you through a series of concrete steps to create and implement a powerful and reliable Year-End Drive at your organization. Those steps, in chronological order, are:

- The Thanksgiving Thank-A-Thon
- The first year-end appeal letter
- The second year-end appeal letter
- The all-important last four days of the year
- The January follow-up
- The segmentation of donors and major donor meetings

One of my favorite assessments of year-end giving comes from the Network for Good, a leading Internet charitable giving resource. Its groundbreaking study on online giving asserts that "December and Disasters dominate."[2] Though we hinted in Chapter 4 at the tendency of donors to respond to relief efforts for the next earthquake, or hurricane, or tsunami, here we will explore the importance to all nonprofits of the other component of year-end donor engagement: the twelfth and final month of the calendar year.

GRATITUDE IS WHAT YOUR YEAR-END DRIVE IS ALL ABOUT

Remember that old Stevie Wonder song "I Just Called to Say I Love You"? When it came out, millions of couples around the world were moved to reach out and phone each other with new romantic entreaties. In retrospect, the reason seems obvious: From time to time, we need to let the people we cherish know how appreciative we are of them. Yet we often forget to do so.

The same is true of your relationships with donors. Gratitude is what your entire Year-End Drive is all about. It is the operative term behind every one of the calls, e-mails, and postcards you'll be addressing to your donors at this time of year. It is why the proper beginning to your drive is, literally, a Thank-A-Thon: a telephone event with the sole purpose of saying thank you to your donors.[3]

The Thanksgiving Thank-A-Thon

The optimal time to do your Thank-A-Thon is the week before—you guessed it—Thanksgiving. You should consider this week to be the official kickoff of your entire YED, although, as you'll see in a moment, your preparation begins long before the end of November.

Thank-A-Thon participants typically love the calling work because there's no "ask" involved; it's just a call with an emotionally pleasing purpose. Usually a group of board members, staff members, and volunteers will come together, armed with lists (prepared in advance) of whom to call and what to say. A typical call to Joe or Jane Donor might go: "Hello, Jane, I'm a board member [or volunteer or staff member] with Compassionate Food Pantry, and I'm just calling to say thank you for your involvement, for your membership, and for your donations." If you happen to know something unique about the person—perhaps the volunteer just introduced your organization to the local Rotary club or acquired extra food for the pantry—then you would say, "I'm aware that you recently did this [name the activity] and we really appreciate it and want you to know the board realizes it, the staff realizes it, and the volunteers realize it as well."

That's it. If you don't get the person on the line but get a voice-mail instead, you can leave the same thank-you message. Let people know that if they need anything more from the organization they can call your main number and/or visit your website. Both the live conversation and the message are very effective, though if you get the person on the phone you'll also be able to experience the pure sense of gratitude and appreciation your donors so often feel from calls like these. Countless are the times one of my staff members or I have heard a donor say, "Oh my, you're the only organization that's ever called me to say thank you. What a nice thing to do!" It's a genuine act of esteem, and you should see it that way, too. Don't think of it as a contrivance because it's really not. It's just calling people to say thank you.

Before the first call, I recommend you tell all your participants to relax and have fun, and in order for them to do so more easily you should prepare an FAQ sheet for them to consult if the need arises. This way, if they're asked, "How's that campaign going?" or "Are there any volunteer opportunities?" or "What's the annual budget this year?" they'll have good answers at the ready. There is never a bad time to show off your preparation and professionalism, and a thank-you call is no exception. If you have an exciting (free) event on the horizon, it's okay to mention that as well.

As for a day and time for your Thank-A-Thon, I recommend asking staff and volunteer leadership to participate either on a weekend afternoon or a weekday early evening. Three hours is usually the right amount of time for the event, and you can give each caller fifteen to twenty donors to call. Before beginning, have everyone spend ten minutes practicing calls and role playing (i.e., taking turns pretending to be the donor). Usually I'll ask people to bring their cell phones and I'll order a few pizzas. While I realize it's only pizza, I'm always pleased to see what a real morale booster it becomes among the callers, and how it adds to the collegial feeling in the room.

The First Year-End Appeal Letter

Here's another important reason your participants should be at ease as they say thanks on your behalf: The same week you begin your Thank-A-Thon, you should also be mailing out your first of two year-end appeal letters. This way you continue your all-important, year-end fundraising efforts while removing all pecuniary interests from the Thank-A-Thon. With the fast pace of the holidays, if you don't give your donors a few gentle reminders, your appeal is likely to get overlooked. In my experience, one of the top reasons cited by donors for not making a philanthropic gift is simply, "No one asked me to."

I suggest you customize your YED, including your appeal letter, so that it states the exact giving history of that particular donor and inspires the donor to give more. If you've done your cultivation work well, your donors care about your cause and understand the central role that your organization plays in your community. They don't have to be convinced. They are value aligned with your organization, and thus will enjoy receiving detailed letters about your work, with which they identify. This letter should contain emotional stories about selected individuals who have benefited from your programs, as well as the numbers of people who have been served and will be served in the future. A well-constructed appeal letter can reinforce the feeling the donor has of being a part of the organization and its work. For instance, one small nonprofit that ran an after-school program told the moving story, through a progression of photographs, of a young boy named Javier who, despite coming from a severely disadvantaged background, became a statewide chess champion and later returned as a volunteer to the nonprofit that had nurtured him in his youth.

The letter should be personalized and include a reply mechanism. Both your first year-end appeal letter and your second year-end letter should remind donors of the amount of their previous contribution and ask for an amount representing a 50 percent increase. Research indicates that donors want guidance on the type of support your organization is seeking. For example: "We appreciate your gift of $500 last year and ask that you consider a gift of $750 for next year."

The actual components of your mailing should consist of a large envelope, a four- to six-page letter, and a small cost-cut reply envelope. "Cost-cut" means that reply information is printed on the flap of the envelope. To see some cutting-edge thinking about reply cards, go to www.thenonprofitfundraisingsolution.com. I suggest you use a mailing house to produce the components of the mailing and to mail the items. If you can supply your donor spreadsheet, the mailing house will be able to insert in each letter the amount of the donor's previous gift and the amount representing the 50 percent increase. In lieu of a mailing house, you can engage a direct mail temp on-site for a week or so if your staff is overwhelmed.

In addition, a mailing house will run your donor list through the U.S. Postal Service's list correction service. This is a standard service that mailing houses perform. If you don't use a mailing house, the Postal Service will do it for you. Go to pe.usps.com/businessmail101/addressing/checkingaccuracy.htm. There you can find instructions on how to submit a printout of your list and the Postal Service will mark any changes. There is a fee for this service.

Alternatively, NCOALink is a licensed vendor that will run your mailing list through special software that updates addresses for donors who have filed a change-of-address with the post office. The advantage to using NCOALink is that you clean up your list before you mail. You will also know in advance how much it's going to cost you (because a vendor charges by the address). With an ancillary service endorsement you get the same result (a corrected address) after you mail, but you don't know how much you'll pay in fees until after the corrections come back.

Direct mail is surprisingly powerful. A national study by Dunham+Company concluded that "donors are three times likelier to give online in response to a direct-mail appeal than an e-appeal."[4] This means *direct mail is three times more effective than e-mail* at generating an actual donation. While sending e-mail appeals exclusively can be tempting because they are less labor-intensive and cost less in the short term, over the long run they raise less money and do far less in terms of donor retention (the best donors are engaged donors). A coordinated effort combining direct mail and e-mail is certainly best of all.

Consulting your donor database to target lapsed donors is also a good idea. To reach lapsed donors you may want to use a different style of appeal letter. For example, you can write: "We miss you, please come back!" and include an incentive to return. For example: "The first 100 renewed donors will receive a T-shirt with our new logo." If it's membership renewal you seek, you could say, "If you act within the next ten days, you'll enjoy a 25 percent savings on the membership rate."

As my colleague Charlie Whelan, president of the Whelan Group, has said:

> *Many organizations used to broadcast "Dear Friend" mailings to thousands of people—a one-size-fits-all appeal to a broad audience. Today, with prospect identification software and market segmentation strategies in place, you can dice that audience into a great many sub-audiences, giving you the ability to custom-tailor these appeals to each of these distinct sub-audiences and to make those appeals in a highly personalized way.*[5]

The donor database is an essential tool in tracking all kinds of relevant information, from addresses to amount of contact and level of mobility. Nonprofits often overlook having an appropriate database because they either think it's unaffordable or they have a general technology phobia. Without a well-maintained database, though, targeting lapsed donors and segmenting major donors is going to be tough or even impossible to implement. Thankfully, there are many solutions readily available even to the most economically challenged nonprofits. Salesforce.com is a great starting point for many non-profits looking to track constituents, partners, donors, donations, activities, volunteers, and cases (though it is labor-intensive and has a significant learning curve). The platform software licenses are free for many nonprofits. The Salesforce Foundation donates up to ten free licenses to each nonprofit, and there are many other free databases available online as well. In the worst case, you can always use an Excel spreadsheet. To quote Peter Drucker once again, "If you can't measure it, you can't manage it."

Through the use of a donor database, you will gain an understanding of donors' giving history based on their contributions to other nonprofits as well as to similar causes within your region. You will also come to understand their capacity to give. Many of these third-party databases offer packages that allow you to bundle services according to your organization's specific need and capacity to spend.

Following is a list of various free and fee-based resources that may help your organization gauge a donor's giving potential. In the free category, school alumni directories are also an excellent resource. Any of these resources can be extremely useful, and most of them provide actual charitable giving histories rather than just giving potentials.

Free Sources
www.tray.com (political donations)
www.opensecrets.org (political donations)
www.hoovers.com (limited free searches on individuals and companies)
www.corporateinformation.com (limited searches on companies)
www.sec.gov (information on board members and executive compensation, including bonuses, retirement plans, and fringe benefits)
www.muckety.com (maps relationships and "influences")
www.martindale.com (attorney information)
www.ama-assn.org (American Medical Association's doctor finder)
www.anybirthday.com (public records database)
www.streeteasy.com (real estate information)

Fee-Based Sources

www.iwave.com (prospect research online)

www.nozasearch.com (NOZAsearch database of charitable donations)

www.blackbaud-analytics.com (prospect research and wealth identification services by Blackbaud)

www.lexisnexis.com/en-us/products/ln-development-professionals.page (LexisNexis for the development professional)

www.wealthengine.com (wealth intelligence platform)

www.larkspurdata.com (DataMaster Pro from Larkspur Data Resources)

Don't forget to post your year-end appeal letter on your website so that donors can make their contributions online as well. Your DONATE Now button should be prominent and visible on all pages of your site. There are sample year-end appeal letters available at www.thenonprofitfundraisingsolution.com.

The Second Year-End Appeal Letter

The next step in your YED is the second year-end appeal letter (or letters), which typically goes out sometime between the first and the third week of December. You may want to have more than one version of the year-end letter to send to the different segments of your donors. There are some nonprofits that will continue mailing letters if they don't hear back from a donor, though most send just one year-end letter. It is critical that you update your database so that donors who responded to your first appeal letter aren't resolicited.

It's always a good idea to freshen up your second year-end letter with new highlights and, of course, make any adjustments necessary based on the changing nature of your cause. If you offer, say, a special holiday meal at Thanksgiving or Christmas, you'll want to mention those events at their appropriate times.

Once you send out your year-end appeal letter, and after thirty days have elapsed without a response, you should supplement it with a "Haven't Heard from You ..." postcard reminder. This step alone can increase your donations by as much as 10 percent. The postcard should contain the website link where the appeal is posted, and ask the donor to go there to learn more and donate.

When planning your YED, think about what you have to celebrate: amazing client outcomes, new funding, new board members, a magical "success" story, news about your cause, and so forth. In conveying this news, you want to make the link between these events and your donors' giving so that donors feel good about giving to you. While letting them know how much you've accomplished, let them also know how much more there is to do and what that will cost.

The Last Four Days of the Year Online Are the Most Important

As mentioned at the start of this chapter, approximately one out of every three dollars in annual giving is donated during the month of December.[6] This powerful concentration of giving amplifies even further as New Year's approaches. The last four days of the year are the biggest, with giving literally quintupling over the course of the last two days. We even know that the peak period on December 31 is between 11:00 a.m. and 7:00 p.m. in whatever time zone the donor happens to be in.

What fuels this surge of beneficence is the ubiquitous reinforcement of the holiday giving spirit, coupled with the pressing need for donors to lock in a tax deduction for the fiscal year. So how best to make use of these remarkably specific statistics? To begin with, you'll want to send an e-mail to your donors on December 28 letting them know to expect another e-mail from you every day for the next four days (in which you'll be telling stories that highlight your organization's successes over the past year). Each of your e-mails can share an aspect of your program's impact that may be little known or frequently overlooked, or perhaps a description of what makes your service unique. Another option is to tell four client stories, one per day, in great detail, about how your services made a positive impact. I worked with one social services provider of youth programs who told the story of the organization's partnership with a local community college. College students would volunteer at the nonprofit to help the youths with homework and recreational activities, with the program then culminating in two weekend camping trips. The nonprofit's Year-End Drive e-mails contained photos from the trips, as well as portraits of younger and older kids together in a heartwarming mentorship setting.

A graphic designer to help create your appeal, and vibrant clear photographs to illustrate it, can help immeasurably. Your own storytelling options will, of course, vary, but your donors will be glad for this concentrated period of cultivation and outreach. One last bit of advice: When it's time to send your final e-mail of the year, I suggest not sending out appeals on December 31 until 11:00 a.m. or 11:30 a.m. Since e-mail programs such as Constant Contact or MailChimp allow you to see when your recipients have actually read your e-mails, you can send a second e-mail around 3:00 p.m. to those who haven't yet opened their morning e-mail.

Be sure you mention your December 31 fundraising deadline, and remind your donors that if their donation envelope is postmarked by that date, their gift qualifies as a tax-deductible contribution for that year, even if it is received after New Year's. For appeals sent by direct mail, write TIME SENSITIVE on the outer envelope.

JANUARY IS THE NEXT BEST TIME OF YEAR FOR GIVING

The last phase of your YED actually takes place in January. Not everyone will respond to your YED, often because they are away on vacation or simply too busy during the holidays. That's why you want to reach out to all your nonresponders just after the holiday season ends. This is also an excellent time to follow up by phone and personally thank the top 20 percent of your donors with a friendly "Happy New Year." Ideally, your board members can help with those calls, but the development staff and the development committee members must lead the way.

Another important January agenda item is to promptly send out tax receipts. While tax considerations are not the main motivator for most donors, they are important, especially for larger donors. Donors will appreciate you reminding them to claim the credits they've earned.

What About Donor Fatigue or Getting Lost in the Shuffle?

I know many well-meaning nonprofits wonder if so many calls, letters, and reminders from their organization might somehow turn off potential donors. My experience is that if donors can't give, they will tell you so, or simply refrain from writing a check. Usually it's because they don't have discretionary income at the time or they are committed to other priorities. These donors may love your organization and mission, but with so many competing interests, they must be reminded of your need and how much revenue is required to solve the problem(s) you're pitching.

Because a significant number of donors don't increase their giving due to their concern that their money will not be spent effectively, you need to think about who your donors are and what they are most interested in knowing about your organization. Your annual report and financial statements should be available to donors who request it. The more transparent and specific you are with them, the better. Would the addition of a new service enable the program to serve more clients? Would one additional staff member make it possible to extend hours or open a longed-for new facility?

Tell your donors how important they are to you and how much they are appreciated. Instead of a generic "Have you given lately?" or "Have you remembered us this year?" donors should be asked to solve specific problems. The basic equation is, Will you help us do X by giving $Y? Here's an example drawn from real life: "The cost of the new dental chair that we need is $5,000. Your last gift of $250 was appreciated, and if you could increase this year's gift to $375, it will go toward the purchase of that chair, and give a brighter smile to a poor child."

Surveying Your Donors

The exact frequency of contacting and reminding your donors until they give is for you to decide, but know that you are probably inclined to ask less than you should, so try to counteract that tendency. One simple and vastly underused way to help ensure that you are reaching out to your donors in the way they desire is to query them through a donor survey. Donors commonly say they did not increase a gift because they disliked the way they were asked for it.

Among the things a donor survey can reveal are preferred means of communication (e.g., phone, e-mail, snail mail) as well as preferred times (evenings, weekends). If you then integrate this information into your database and respect your donors' expressed wishes, you and your staff can limit the risk of irritating the people you are hoping to connect with. Consider including a donor survey in your development plan or even in your year-end appeal.

DONOR MEETINGS TO DISCUSS MAJOR GIFTS

In Chapter 3, I referred to the 80/20 rule, which says that 80 percent of your funding typically comes from about 20 percent of your donors. This rule especially comes into play as part of your YED because it is the optimum time of year to discuss major gifts during your personal donor meetings. These donors are the people whose donations will spearhead your year-end campaign, and they require a much higher degree of personalized attention when appealed to. By Labor Day, you should have finished segmenting your donors; then sometime between mid-October and mid-December you should begin preparing to set up meetings with your largest donors: the top 20 percent of your givers.

Typically, I'll write to or call my top 20 percent and say, "I'd like to meet and update you about the organization and talk about your year-end gift." Some donors are so accustomed to it after all these years that they'll occasionally reply, "We don't need to meet this year." However, if that's the case, I don't recommend just abandoning the conversation right there. It still behooves you to ask, "What would work for you this year?" If you have a challenge gift (as discussed in Chapter 7), this phone call would be an appropriate time to let them know about it. If you feel a year-end gift is just not in the cards from a particular donor, you can still suggest a no-obligations meeting to update the person about the organization.

It typically takes more time to secure larger gifts, since donors must plan a large gift more meticulously because of the implications for their year-end tax planning. Given the potential for their year-end largesse, though, you should be devoting extra time and planning on your end to segment and work with these donors. Know who your loyal donors are. Communicate with them differently from others who have supported you only once or twice, or whose support is more sporadic. If you treat your loyal donors carefully, you can build an enduring relationship with them that can lead to larger gifts over time.

AT THE END OF THE DAY

No time of the year is as important to a fundraiser as the last two months of the year. Nonprofits receive one of every three dollars donated in the month of December alone; no other month even comes close. Thanks to the warm holiday spirit and donors needing to lock in their charitable tax credits for the year, the end of the year is when the lion's share of charitable giving takes place. There are a host of proven techniques to use, including the Thanksgiving Thank-A-Thon, the first year-end appeal letter, the second year-end appeal letter, the last four days of the year e-mail drive, the January follow-up, and the segmentation of donors and major donor meetings. Adopting these techniques as part of your annual year-end appeal can increase giving to your organization exponentially.

CHAPTER NINE

FUNDRAISING AND RELATIONSHIP BUILDING THROUGH SOCIAL MEDIA

CUTTING-EDGE, UBIQUITOUS, AND REMARKABLY POWERFUL, social media possesses a "wow" factor that is unmatched by any development in fundraising over the last fifty years, if not more. Nothing even comes close. In the area of disaster relief alone, text message, Twitter, and Facebook social media campaigns have proved to be legitimate fundraising juggernauts, raising tens of millions of dollars seemingly overnight.

Yet the tendency to look at social media primarily as a cash cow is inaccurate and misses much of the real point about how social media can advance your nonprofit. While it's true that the primarily large, well-known nonprofits with recognizable brands, such as the American Red Cross and the Susan G. Komen Breast Cancer Foundation, have smashed records through social media fundraising, lesser-known groups have had moderate social media fundraising success, too. One such nonprofit is charity: water. Others have been equally or more successful using social media outside the immediate fundraising function, in areas such as constituency building and large-scale messaging. This is exactly the type of relationship building that should be central to your fundraising plan because it enhances your future fundraising potential. That's not to say that things won't change and that social media fundraising won't become your primary "ask" tool, but for now it is better understood as an active, evolving, and multifaceted medium for the long term rather than a glittering, diamond-encrusted panacea of instant riches.

Authors such as Beth Kanter and Allison Fine, who cowrote *The Networked Nonprofit*,[1] have extensively and intelligently covered how to use social media in and of itself. What I'll focus on in this chapter is how social media can be used as a *relational component* of your overall fundraising strategy. A large part of what we do in fundraising—both online and offline—is not immediately or directly related to collecting donations. Throughout the book I've discussed strategies and tactics that have nothing to do with getting a check in the first (or second or third) interaction and everything to do with building a relationship to further your fundraising goals in the future. Social media fits neatly into this pattern for relationship building. Fundraising is a relationship business; it's about people, and that doesn't change when the people are sitting behind their computers or scouring social media platforms on their cell phones.

In this chapter we'll explore:
- How to get started with social media
- Seven questions to determine how well your social media fundraising is working
- The indirect value of social media in fundraising
- How to integrate social media into your existing fundraising methods
- Four simple ways to use social media to fundraise

There is a counterintuitive nature to social media that mirrors several of the higher performance themes we explored in Part One. For example, if you want to speak with other people on Twitter, you must first "follow" them rather than lead the conversation, an echo of the good followership concept that we explored in Chapter 2. Similarly, on Facebook and other platforms throughout the blogosphere, readers' comments are as vigorous and valuable as the initial posted message. In other words, listening can be just as important as speaking. This "pulling" quality of social media, in which feedback equals or exceeds the input or "push" of your message, also indicates that another dynamic is at work—namely, humility (which you may recognize from Chapter 2 as one of our keys to good leadership). As we explore social media in this chapter, I hope you'll seek to understand it as something both new and old. Let's examine why.

GETTING STARTED WITH SOCIAL MEDIA

Perhaps you want to increase awareness of your agency among women through a predominantly female social media platform like Pinterest. Maybe you want to start an online dialogue about funding cuts and how to avoid them. Or possibly you just want to participate in leading-edge discussions of your mission online. Typically, training your staff and volunteers to use social media effectively, as with any new technology, would be the most costly element in achieving any of these goals. However, these days computers and social media are such an integral part of everyday life that almost everyone has some experience they can bring to bear, and therefore basic training costs can be vastly mitigated. While experience counts in the social media realm, young people especially tend to be open to and adept at using the various tools of the trade. They may, as a matter of course, wake up texting, check their Facebook and Twitter accounts throughout the day, and sleep while still logged into Skype.

To get in step with the technological present, you need individuals familiar and comfortable with social media tools and platforms. A larger organization, of course, can outsource technology and social media training. If you are a small organization, you might just begin by asking who among your group has the most experience with Facebook, Twitter, or blogging and build from there. Alternately, you can form a social media committee and recruit a team of appropriately skilled volunteers to it.

In any event, before you make any major investment, it is critical that you identify your objectives, a task that can initially seem elusive with social media.

SEVEN QUESTIONS TO DETERMINE HOW WELL YOUR SOCIAL MEDIA FUNDRAISING IS WORKING

As with any of your other strategic decisions, your time spent on social media requires thoughtful cost-benefit and ROI forecasts to assess its strengths and weaknesses. This assessment can be especially complex, because the metrics for social media are different and not always easy to quantify.

As we've seen in Chapter 6, a parlor gathering might cost X dollars to put on and bring in Y dollars in new donations and Z number of new prospects. How do you compare these types of traditional metrics to, say, 20,000 hits on your agency's most recent blog post or 160,000 monthly page views on your Facebook page? What does it mean that your agency's last tweet was retweeted 900 times? The truth is, there is no simple answer, and you may sometimes feel as though you are comparing apples to oranges.

However, there are seven questions to ask about your use of social media that can guide you in creating your own metrics of success:

1. Is it increasing your donor prospect base, and by how much?
2. Is it increasing your donor conversion rate, and by how much?
3. How long will it take to recoup the costs of piloting or upgrading your social media program?
4. Is your use of social media increasing your transactional efficiency (i.e., are you reducing costs per donation or per new volunteer)?
5. Is it expanding internal capacity and training, and if so, by how much?
6. Is your message reaching more people and do you have more "influencers" (aka "thought leaders") in cyberspace spreading your message?
7. Is it leading to increased giving?

You may recognize that these questions are essentially the same sort of metrics you apply to any of your fundraising strategies. What's different is that whereas with a fundraising newsletter, for instance, you can determine its cost in terms of time, printing, and mailing, and measure that against its return (new donors, new prospects, new clients), social media initiatives behave differently. Someone reads your post, comments on it, and e-mails or tweets it to another person or group. These other people in turn "like" it and repost it, after it is commented on by a new reader, and then you, and so on, potentially ad infinitum. This is the beauty of "viral" media; the number of interactions they can lead to is limitless, and proliferate often at breathtaking speed. But it also means the value of each initiative needs to be placed less on direct response and more on interactivity.

Of all the seven questions, the most important may be your conversion rate, because ultimately you are hoping to convert more and more prospects to becoming donors. But, as mentioned previously, if you are only looking at social media for its immediate ROI, you are missing the point about its potential impact for your organization. The possibilities of using social media for other purposes—to have a robust online conversation about your cause in which your organization is seen as an "influencer," for instance, or an online convergence among nonprofits like yours to develop common initiatives—can be just as important as a cluster of new donors. You are still essentially fundraising through your social media (i.e., seeking conversion), but like many of the fundraising tactics I've discussed (donor meetings, cultivation tours of your agency, and so on), you are doing so by building relationships that lead to giving. Social media, *in the service of your fundraising,* has the potential to expand the number, impact, and reach of those relationships by several orders of magnitude.

THE VALUE OF SOCIAL MEDIA BEYOND FUNDRAISING

That last point cannot be overstated. In 2012, a nonprofit called Invisible Children launched a social media campaign known as KONY 2012 to bring attention to the atrocities perpetrated in Central Africa by the so-called Lord's Resistance Army, led by the notorious warlord Joseph Kony. Within weeks, tens of millions of viewers around the world watched a YouTube video about Kony, and the story went viral across a multitude of online platforms. A movement to bring Kony to justice was born online, seemingly in an instant. This is but one example of the power of social media to build awareness and relationships among like-minded people and organizations.

In the information age, information is capital. Just as we recognize fundraising ROI in the nonprofit world, we must begin to seek and accept what might be called *informational ROI.* By this I mean something akin to what are called "eyeballs" in traditional media. How many people are seeing, hearing, and being reached by your message? How many of your primary targets are being "hit," as it were? Because of social media's ability to reach audiences broadly or to target them precisely, it presents a truly fresh and unique mechanism to transact informational capital.

Let's say your organization is dedicated to finding a cure for multiple myeloma. Through the blogosphere, you can readily identify and reach patients, survivors, bloggers, physicians, pharmaceutical companies, and other thought leaders and constituents directly concerned with your same issue. At the same time, on a vastly broader scale, you can also connect with the National Institutes of Health and its equivalents throughout the world. As you tweet, post, blog, or otherwise take part in the conversation (as leader or follower), you are continually building your public identity and elevating the credibility of your agency and cause. You are also laying the groundwork for your future fundraising.

But social media and a modern technology strategy require a different mental approach as well. Just as you were asked to consider higher-level thinking in Chapter 4, a similar change in thinking should accompany technology strategy and social media work at your agency. For example, as we learn to value pull and push equally, traditional proprietary thinking must give way to what's commonly called "open source" behavior; that is, rather than husbanding information and treating it as proprietary (e.g., "Our planned giving strategy is a secret"), you are sharing and comparing it and exposing your work and ideas to like-minded individuals and groups. By doing so, you are not only spreading your ideas but simultaneously learning about yourself, gathering constructive criticism, and honing your message and mission. For all its chatter, social media is very much about group listening. You put your ideas out and listen for reactions, suggestions, comments, and an overall deepening of the conversation. You "pull" as you "push." At the same time, you'll want to tie this "honing" process into your existing technology architecture.

FURTHER INTEGRATING SOCIAL MEDIA INTO YOUR EXISTING FUNDRAISING SYSTEMS

As with any new technology, a smart social media plan should be integrated into your existing fundraising program. For instance, every nonprofit needs to manage its relations with constituents. There's customer relationship management (CRM) software that does that, which we touched on in Chapter 5. Large nonprofits often build their own CRM system from scratch, or they might pay for a proprietary service like Blackbaud. But there are free CRMs like CiviCRM, SugarCRM, or Salesforce.com as well. You are also going to need a content management system (CMS) that maintains your website, which Blackbaud also offers, as well as open source providers like Concrete5 and many others. The goal is to link all these systems modules seamlessly: your CRM with your CMS, with your accounting software, with your online efforts. What becomes proprietary to you is no longer the technology itself but the manner in which you knit these elements together.

Social media can be thought of as third-party software that enables your audience not only to communicate with you but *among themselves,* which is one of the main ways your message moves outward, spreading beyond your initial, narrower targets. Your existing systems then manage the relationship between your Facebook friends and, say, your constituent addresses so that when you get a new friend on Facebook that information is entered into your CRM data. That person will automatically get a letter of introduction generated through your e-mail contact provider or your own website, or perhaps automatically receive your annual appeal through snail mail.

Having social media integrated into your existing fundraising program can help reduce costs, though obviously the bigger impact of social media is that it can dramatically increase your scale by many multiples of your costs. It enables a small group to reach a proportion that prior technologies could not. A small group with the right small idea that employs social media technology effectively can become very big, very fast.

FOUR SIMPLE WAYS TO FUNDRAISE THROUGH SOCIAL MEDIA

As mentioned at the outset of this chapter, technology tools and the ways they are used will inevitably change, and more people may start giving more directly through social media sites. For the foreseeable future, the two most important characteristics of a strong social media program are constant activity (since nothing looks worse than pages and conversations that haven't been updated for months) and integration between your online efforts and the more traditional tactics you continue to do offline.

The breakneck speed of change in technology and the ever-growing scrap heap of moribund "next big thing" platforms (such as Myspace) can understandably leave even the most technologically eager agency scratching its institutional head and wondering which way to direct its social media fundraising efforts. Thus far, a fundraising drive on Facebook, the largest social media platform in the world, is unlikely to net your nonprofit big money (the average online monthly donation at the time of writing is only $32).[2] On the other hand, DonorsChoose, an online charity that funds public school classroom projects, has raised more than $101 million online through its website and social media initiatives.[3] While it's still tough to predict which, if any, social media platforms will lead to immediate fundraising gains, your continuous online presence will almost certainly lead to more money when you make your more traditional appeals via e-mail, phone, or face-to-face meetings. Through your presence online, as with any other fundraising outreach, you are building and deepening relationships. This also underlines why it's so important to see your social media and online efforts as gears in your fundraising engine, and not the engine itself.

Here are four simple ways to begin to use online platforms to enable fundraising in your overall strategy:

1. *Get followers to sign up for your e-mail list.* Most online donations are made through an organization's website, and e-appeals bring in significant returns. As a fan of your Facebook page or a follower on Twitter, a donor is more likely to sign up for your e-mails and give you the opportunity to present them with well-crafted solicitations.

2. *Recruit volunteers through social media.* If you can get volunteers through social media—in-person or virtual volunteers—these individuals will be more likely to donate to your cause. People look to social media for opportunities to get more involved.

3. *Seek social media sponsorships.* When you develop a large enough social media presence or have a particular niche, you

can negotiate sponsorship deals from companies that want access to your following (e.g., an outerwear company as a sponsor of the American Canyon Society).

4. *Create donor matches for Shares/Likes/Retweets.* Ask a major donor who understands the importance of spreading the word about your cause for a gift that matches each share, like, or retweet you receive online. This strategy helps you both spread the word and bring in needed funding.

Though the world of technology is constantly changing, it's worth remembering the popular French expression *plus ça change, plus c'est la même chose* (translation: the more things change, the more they stay the same). The basic tenets of advanced fundraising haven't become obsolete just because nonprofit fundraising employs social media. As you explore different ways to make social media channels work best for your organization, including direct fundraising, remember that your road to higher revenues still is and always will be built on the relationships you are able to create as well as deepen. Social media allows you to raise your own self-awareness as it raises awareness of your agency in others. For these reasons and more, it merits your considered and immediate embrace.

AT THE END OF THE DAY

Social media is one component of your overall fundraising plan, which is in turn linked to all your fundraising through relationship building. Social media's fundraising prowess is formidable, though for smaller organizations its true promise lies in its ability to establish a powerful public identity for you and your mission and to create new relationships. Using an "open source" approach to social media allows you to grow stronger as you and your mission grow more connected and widely known. Even if you can't yet raise big money through social media, you can use it to enhance your future fundraising. It's best to embrace communications and fundraising strategies that integrate online and offline channels.

CHAPTER TEN

FORMING POWERFUL LEADERSHIP COUNCILS

THROUGHOUT THIS BOOK WE'VE DISCUSSED a host of different ways to increase fundraising for your nonprofit. One of the best ways, though not always the easiest, is a special power that all charities possess; a trait that is often overlooked even though it is shared with, among others, the Wizard of Oz. I'm talking about the power to convey legitimacy upon others. This is done in the nonprofit world through leadership councils.

A leadership council is a group of individuals outside of your board (though some of them may also be board members) who fulfill a number of special functions for your agency. Unlike your board members who assume a governance responsibility, the council is a nongovernance group. Someone once said to me, "The difference between my board and my council is that my board is for heavy lifting; the council only does light lifting." In other words, you may not need the entire House of Representatives; you just need a special committee to get on the bandwagon.

There is a certain magic, if you will, that exists in all nonprofits, and that comes along with the distinction of "working for a good cause." Though nonprofit work is frequently nonremunerative, people who are associated with a charity can at least carry their head high because they are ennobled by the high-mindedness and positive impact of their mission on people's lives. As a result, each organization is inherently endowed with an ability to extend that high-mindedness to others through mutual association. Just as the grandiloquent Wizard conferred intellectual sanction on the Scarecrow by presenting him with an honorary doctorate in "Thinkology," a nonprofit has myriad strategic ways to externally gather and convey legitimacy, usually in the service of fundraising, though often with the additional purpose of achieving important goals that fall outside of the board's purview or ability.

In this chapter, we'll examine:
- What a leadership council does
- What to name your council
- Situations best served by a leadership council
- How to recruit and work with your leadership council

Through leadership councils, not only can your organization facilitate service, it can share its prestige while simultaneously basking in the spotlight of others, thus raising your profile in your community—all free of charge.

WHAT A LEADERSHIP COUNCIL DOES

Depending on the type of council you empower, a leadership council can enable you to achieve any number of goals: fundraise, deal with community politics, offer or facilitate access to expertise, write letters advocating or defending on your behalf, or sometimes simply provide a healthy dose of ex officio credibility for your agency.

One of the most common uses of a council is that it can act as a liaison with the community at large, though usually in a directed and less public-relations-intensive way than might be done through a regular board or marketing initiative. For instance, a group of doctors might provide testimony at public hearings about health issues (e.g., diabetes prevention, air pollution) at the behest of the nonprofit on whose council they serve. They could endorse the work that the nonprofit is doing, or simply act on behalf of the nonprofit as experts on the topic at hand. In either case, this public platform increases their own credibility while simultaneously enhancing the image of the nonprofit they represent. It's a perfect win-win.

WHAT TO NAME YOUR COUNCIL

Just as there are numerous tasks that a leadership council can success-fully undertake, there are several different ways to name your council to make it attractive and give it direction. "Friends of ..." is general enough to fit many designations, and what's especially nice about this moniker is that it immediately tells a story. Friends help someone in need, and do so out of love and friendship (i.e., without ulterior mo-tives). Sometimes you'll want to set up an "honorary council." You can have presidents councils, volunteer councils, fundraising coun-cils, or any number of "task forces" (on gun violence, coastal preser-vation, bedbugs in public housing, and so forth).

Depending on the need and the type of members you hope to attract, an appropriate designation can be crafted in whichever way you feel will best serve you and your organization. The point is to think through which name best reflects your reason for establishing the council and select that one. If in doubt, you can test the name out on a few people you trust before deciding.

SITUATIONS BEST SERVED BY A LEADERSHIP COUNCIL

Just as there are numerous labels for the various types of leadership councils, there are endless ways in which the creation of a leadership council can help your nonprofit. Here are a few situations you may not have thought of or yet encountered.

Acquisition or Merger

When two organizations mesh as one, either through acquisition or merger, their new board doesn't necessarily have to just double in size. Everyone may not be a perfect fit for the new board, though you don't want the board members from the smaller or less power-ful of the two original organizations to just drift off into the sun-set or feel as if their usefulness has expired. On the contrary, you'll want to keep them engaged even if they are no longer carrying out board governance work.

This very situation arose when two environmental organizations merged. One was especially strong in knowing which on-the-ground programs worked well to mobilize people in support of the environment, while the other nonprofit's strengths lay in its leadership, power, and access to money.

The new CEO, having determined that her new board was sufficiently large, had to decide what to do with a whole group of board members who had been enormously helpful to both organizations in the past, and whom she wanted to keep involved in a meaningful way with the new entity. She also had to, ahem, move some people around who weren't quite right for the new board.

Her solution was to create a Presidents Council for them to serve on. Among other things, the council members could be responsible for maintaining the "institutional memory" of the previous organizations: how they did things in the past, how various capital campaigns worked out and why, and so forth. The members of the Presidents Council continued to enjoy the esteem of appearing on the group's letterhead, and at the same time felt their contributions were still most welcome.

When You Need to Fly Under the Radar

Very often, situations will arise in the communities where you operate that require an especially delicate touch. Say you run a Planned Parenthood clinic in an area that is hostile to your presence for political or religious reasons. You may want to weigh in on funding hearings to prevent STDs without necessarily drawing attention to your organization and every service it provides. This could be the ideal situation for you to create a Doctors (or Nurses) Council, whose purpose is to not only deflect negative attention from your nonprofit, but actually highlight other lesser-known preventive services you provide to the community at large.

Likewise, if you were a faith-based nonprofit looking to take part in a community dialogue about the Middle East, a Rabbis and Imams Council might better focus attention on your organization's religious views instead of your perceived political affiliations.

At times, you may even have a reason to fly under your own radar. For example, if you find yourself in the midst of a board crisis, members of a leadership council can reassure others (e.g., funders, politicians) that it's just a bump in the road and all will be well. A "Friends of ..." council can be up and running in as little as a few months.

Garnering Greater Representation in Your Community

Most of the councils I have been a member of or helped form ranged in size from a dozen to forty people, but the size of the council will always depend on the agency's particular needs. For instance, I once visited a nonprofit that I'll call the Upper Coast County Association. It represented a population of several million, had 55 people on its board of directors, and 200 people on its Community Council. When I asked the CEO why his board and council were so large, he replied, "Look at my name! I'm the Upper Coast County Association. If I don't have all the main players from business, government, and nonprofit on my board or council, I'll never get anything done because when I take initiatives, I need *everybody* behind me."

In a similar vein, you might be a medium or small nonprofit but relatively new in your sector or geographical area. If your letters of introduction go out with a number of prominent community leaders or celebrity names listed on your letterhead under LEADERSHIP COUNCIL, you will draw infinitely more attention to your organization and your cause.

A Major Campaign

One of the best ways to supplement a major fundraising campaign is to establish something like a Citizens Council or a Community Council. The greater people perceive the reach of your initiative to be, the more likely they will want to take part in it, because the prestige they will receive in exchange for their participation will be showcased to a wider audience. Major donors are more likely to want to participate in something that seeks out and validates their wisdom and stature, not just solicits their money. A council does just that.

Unlike when you create your board, you are free from legal and procedural strictures in creating leadership councils. All leadership councils are different, with varying rules, obligations, and life spans. You can custom-fit yours to your particular agency and task, though to do so successfully, you need to keep it simple and focused on a few strategic goals, and you need to put energy into maintaining and growing it. Many councils die prematurely of neglect.

HOW TO RECRUIT AND WORK WITH YOUR LEADERSHIP COUNCIL

The first step in recruiting council members is to clearly define what it is you are expecting of them, both in terms of time commitment and ultimate goals. Remember that anyone you approach is going to be, in all likelihood, a busy person, and people have their own time obligations. I recommend that you identify clear, tangible goals to convey to each of your council prospects (e.g., "We want passage of this particular piece of new legislation in the next election," or "We need to raise $1 million to build our new facility next year"), along with a set amount of hours and meetings you expect from them each quarter or biannually, depending on the nature of the goal. As Kim Klein, copublisher of the *Grassroots Fundraising Journal,* says, "A good question to ask yourself is whether you would agree to serve on such an advisory board."[1] Bear in mind, however, that your capabilities and schedule may not be the same as those of the people you approach.

There are many groups of individuals who would make good candidates for your council. When recruiting, consider:

- People who have made a contribution to your board in the past, but for whom you no longer have a structure in place to keep them involved in the same capacity.
- Those who would like to be associated with your organization but don't have sufficient time to carry out the duties of a trustee.
- Individuals you are fond of who have competing interests with your organization that preclude them from becoming a trustee. They can still possibly lend an endorsement, through the vehicle of a leadership council.

Before you reach out to anyone, it's advisable to create a list of characteristics you want and need (which are not the same thing) from the individuals on your board. For instance, for a council dedicated to the passage of legislation, you might want your members to have some legal background, though what you absolutely need are individuals who are comfortable speaking in public. Again, these criteria will vary from council to council and task to task, but proper delineation of your wants and needs ahead of time will significantly expedite and clarify the entire recruitment process.

Recruiting Council Members

When creating any type of leadership council, the first recruitment step (after you've outlined your wish list of characteristics and made a list of prospects in consultation with your board) is to reach out to your prospects by phone and see if they are interested. You don't want to meet with someone who hasn't the time or inclination to take part. If a prospect is amenable to your proposal, arrange to meet in person. It is advisable to bring at least one other person to that meeting, just as you would for a major gift meeting, to provide additional perspective and to help answer any questions the prospect may have. Although you've reached out to your prospect, as opposed to him or her having contacted you, you should still regard this meeting as an interview for a (volunteer, unremunerated) job position. Do you think this person will work well in this capacity? Is the person enthusiastic about achieving results and comfortable committing time? As a rule, it is far better to be disappointed now, rather than later. There may be other councils formed in the future that are better suited to this individual.

Suppose a prospect doesn't return your call? Should you wait for a response or move on? I suggest you try calling three times — with two days in between each call—and afterward send a personal handwritten note saying you've been trying to reach the person and asking if he or she would please call you. If the prospect still doesn't call after a week or two, it's time to move on to your next candidate.

Fundraising councils can recruit from almost anywhere, as long as the members it recruits are somehow connected to potentially new financial resources. But just because people are wealthy or know other wealthy individuals does not mean they will make good fundraisers, the same way that having money does not make a person proficient at earning it (often the case with those who inherit wealth). While all fundraisers brought onto your fundraising council needn't be wealthy, they will all need to be comfortable asking others for money or making introductions for that specific purpose. What you are looking for on a fundraising council are individuals who can effectively approach and persuade potential funders (individuals, corporations, or foundations) and who possess the connections to readily reach out to them.

The ability to host a fundraising event at their home or business is another excellent qualification. If the prospective council members are wealthy and want to lead by example, all the better; in fact, it's almost mandatory that they be willing to give generously if they have the means—otherwise their solicitations to others are likely to ring hollow.

Working with Council Members

If your initial interviews go well and you elect to appoint the prospects to the council, they can begin working almost immediately. You can also decide to appoint one or more people as cochairs for your council and begin once you have them on board. To reiterate, you do not have any sort of quorum requirements as you might with a board, and each subsequent council member you appoint can augment the work already begun. You may decide to wait until you have several council members on board; depending on the task and time frame, this may be a more prudent course. But your options are far greater than they are when choosing your board. Practically speaking, when you've received verbal consent from prospective council members, you will need to send them a letter of invitation to memorialize their consent to participate. Remember, you ask them in person, and you formalize that invitation after they've accepted, by mail. At some point, usually by the time of your first meeting, you'll want to present them with a list of whatever council membership requirements you've created, as well as any and all benefits of being part of the council, such as having their name appear on your letterhead and website.

A good next step is to host an initial gathering, possibly a tour of your agency if appropriate, where you will also announce the date for the annual council meeting. Once your council is up and running, you should check in with the council members regularly, keep them up to speed on all organizational developments, and take an active oversight role regarding upcoming deadlines, results benchmarks, or any problems that may be brewing among the members.

The main purpose of any council is to allow an organization to delegate a task or tasks that it doesn't have the capacity or means to address. In an ideal world, your council members will be able to coalesce and act as a leading edge of your organizational vessel. However, at least one person, even a volunteer, should be charged with liaising between the council(s) and the CEO so as to be sure the former is sufficiently engaged and up to speed. A lack of engagement or a feeling of irrelevancy can doom a council to, dare I say, disengaged irrelevancy. One excellent way to boost council participation and cohesiveness is to occasionally invite a guest speaker to address them. As your councils develop, so too will your ideas for honing and strengthening them.

Board members can be invited to the annual meetings of the leadership councils, and you can also occasionally ask a council member or two to attend board meetings. How exactly your board and council interact is up to you and your board. You should also establish how your nominating process for your council will take place now and in the future.

Be they honorary councils, "friends of" committees, or president's councils, here are the bare minimum requirements to consider when forming your next leadership council:

- A few people will put time in to nurture, care, and feed the group.
- An annual meeting date is set a year ahead.
- There's a commitment on the part of the coordinators to meet once a year with each member personally or by phone to update council members and define their roles.
- Recruitment of new members is an ongoing routine task.
- There's a clear, substantial, and concrete purpose.

CONFER AND USE YOUR LEGITIMACY WISELY

Legitimacy, whether conferred by or upon you, is based on respect through association. It's similar to the way a prospective employer checks an applicant's job references. A leadership council is a group of people who effectively say, through their association, "We've checked this group's references and they're solid." As you can see in Figure 10-1, the legitimacy you convey upon your appointees in turn endows them with the bona fides of your organization. Therefore, as with any great power, you are advised to wield it carefully. Credibility is hard-won and extremely valuable, particularly in times of crisis, when a leadership council can literally save your hide by speaking favorably on your behalf.

Figure 10-1. Leadership council chart.

The heart of any leadership council is fostering philanthropy. Two sides come together, a community need and donor resources, to meet that need. The nonprofit organization must make that need crystal clear, and the donor must feel drawn to meet that need. Once the two are brought together, the nonprofit enjoys the power of endorsement that its donors believe in the cause, and the donors in turn enjoy affiliation and recognition with a cause larger than themselves.

⟢ CASEBOOK ⟣

In 1990, I became the new CEO of an unknown nonprofit that was just a few years old. In my first week on the job, a prominent funder told me in no uncertain terms that there was a glut of agencies like ours—agencies with similar missions—and we should seriously consider folding. I was angry. I didn't want to hear we were redundant. But in the quiet of my heart I knew he was right, and I also knew that if this agency was to continue we would have to find a way to distinguish ourselves from the "glut" of others, and do so quickly. The solution, it turned out, was an Honorary Council. How good of a solution was it? Twenty-three years later, that agency is still going, and stronger than ever. The funder had been right, but as they say, not so right that it killed us.

Here were the main aspects of our Honorary Council's evolution:

The Council's Purpose. We acutely needed advocates to distinguish and raise awareness of our agency in the wider community. We knew that community advocacy would keep our organization vibrant and responsive to community needs and build goodwill among our neighbors, political representatives, and prospective new donors. Successful council members helped build our agency's reputation, influence, and funding base. They hosted "parties with a purpose" on our behalf (see Chapter 6) and recruited new members for our various organizational committees. The council's purpose grew over time, not so much by design, although we did have a solid plan in place, but by the enthusiasm the members had for our work.

Naming the Council. We were not fond of the name "advisory board" because both words sent the wrong message: Advice is not what we wanted the group to provide (although we did welcome their input) and we did not want them to be a board in the same way our governing board was. We chose to call it an "Honorary Council" because, by allowing our agency to associate with their names, the council members were honoring us.

The Council's Mission. The mission of an Honorary Council may vary depending on the needs of the organization, but all of the group's members will be charged with helping the organization's external relationships. Our Honorary Council was a nongoverning body designed to boost our agency's public affairs in three broad areas:
- Enhanced networking and goodwill among community members
- Increased credibility among stakeholders "by association with and endorsement of" our agency
- Augmented fundraising efforts, especially fundraising by individual donors

The Council's Structure and Responsibilities. Our council membership consisted of fifty-five prominent individuals from a cross-section of professional fields and areas of expertise. Their names appeared on our agency stationary and annual reports. Members were recruited from the fields of education, finance, and politics, and also included popular figures in politics or entertainment. The council had no governance or fiduciary responsibility. In addition to attending one annual gathering, members were encouraged to host one special annual "party with a purpose" fundraising event at their home or workplace. Six of them—the ones with the best networks—hosted parties, some on an annual basis and others every two years.

Issues for the Council to Address. By answering the following important questions before launching the council, we outlined a structure and procedures to solidify the council's future and its workings vis-à-vis our board:
- To what extent and under what circumstances would the council and the board of directors interact? How would the concept of a new

council be introduced to the board members so as to ensure their input and adoption? We decided to elect council cochairs and invite them to occasionally make presentations at our board meetings.

- Who would staff the council and be responsible for its coordination? How would members be oriented to and continually educated about our agency's mission, goals, and activities? This is a vital step in ensuring that once you establish the council, it does not become dormant as so many similar councils do. We assigned the project management to our development associate and made it 25 percent of his overall job.
- What would our nomination process look like? We assumed that the nomination function would be discharged by our senior staff in the first year, but in subsequent years we moved it to our board's nomination committee. We set criteria for what we were looking for in the group's membership.

Ready, Set, Go. After only two planning meetings, we took these actions, many of which proved to be decisive:
- We created a list of prospective members to get the ball rolling. Rather than censor ourselves, we let the prospects decide if being a council member was amenable to them. The list of candidates was developed with our board.
- We suggested, and then vetted, cochairs for the council, and made gender parity a priority. Gender parity is important for many reasons, including that women are underrepresented in philanthropic leadership. We wanted to send a message about our awareness of and sensitivity to that issue, and open ourselves up to the widest pool of talent as well.
- We had phone conversations with the candidates before we had in-person meetings. We wanted to make sure the person was interested first.
- We mailed invitations for membership to the invitees only after we had their verbal consent that they would join. We invited candidates to a gathering for a tour of our agency.
- We called to follow up the invitation to ensure they would attend and to ask them to bring their spouse or special friend. (We were told that people would be more likely to show if they were coming with a friend or spouse, and this proved to be true.)
- We hosted an initial gathering and secured written commitments for joining the council.
- We then announced the date for the annual council meeting.

- We created a one-page list of council membership requirements and benefits.
- We met once a year to evaluate our work.

The Results. We calculated that our Honorary Council had an annual return of $250,000 within the first two years, and then continued at that level annually for the next three years. The funds came from the members themselves and others they had asked to give. We set annual benchmarks for the fundraising goals of the council based on each member's past giving to us and their (carefully researched) capacity to give. We also documented that the council connected us with government and local leaders, which gained our agency much-needed credibility. This last outcome was actually more important than the cash support because we were unknown at the time and needed to distinguish ourselves.

AT THE END OF THE DAY

Leadership councils by any name consist of a dozen or more respected and admired individuals from a cross-section of professional fields. They don't displace your board of directors because they have no governance or fiduciary responsibility. They compliment the board by augmenting its fundraising efforts, especially with individuals of high net worth. Their names may appear on your letterhead and website, and they will each be encouraged to assume a task of their choosing to advance your mission and goals. Leadership council members may write letters of endorsement, or accompany board members to networking functions, or otherwise open doors and make introductions for you. The council gathers annually to receive an update from the executive director and board president and to exchange ideas. In the meantime, their prestige transfers to your organization and helps to establish its legitimacy and importance. On councils with a fundraising focus, each member should be asked to give a significant gift to the non-profit and to consider hosting a parlor gathering.

CHAPTER ELEVEN

Taking a New Approach to Corporate Sponsorships

CORPORATIONS SPEND AN ESTIMATED $18.7 billion annually on sponsorship in North America alone.[1] What sponsors are looking for is a "meaningful relationship" with consumers, because in the twenty-first century, it is no longer sufficient to merely expose a brand as widely as possible. Thanks to information technology, brands are constantly impinging on our collective consciousness. Most of all, sponsors want to create, enhance, or deepen an emotional connection between consumers and their brand. Though it takes more time and effort to hook a consumer emotionally, studies have shown that doing so ultimately generates more sales than advertising alone.

Here is an example of corporate bonding at work: State Farm Insurance positions itself as "being there" 24/7 for its customers. One year at Thanksgiving, the company provided a free messaging center in malls across the country. Shoppers were invited to send holiday messages to loved ones and even insert photographs of themselves in their message. The purpose of the campaign was not only to demonstrate that "like a good neighbor, State Farm was there." The objective was to stimulate feelings occasioned by the holiday and thoughts of family—feelings that shoppers would thereafter identify with the red and white State Farm logo.

The parallel with the nonprofit process of cultivating individual donors is uncanny. A fundraiser will work with an executive director to create a moment during a site visit or presentation that will bring tears to the eyes of a potential donor. Like the nonprofit professional, the for-profit marketing director understands the power of an emotional identification. Just as it is the key to turning a casual shopper into a lifelong customer, it is the means of turning a casual giver into a lifelong donor.

In this chapter, we'll:

- Take a look at a mathematical formula used to evaluate sponsorship proposals.
- Examine ways that your organization can get in on corporate largesse through the prism of two corporate partnering case studies: one on a national level, the other one local.
- Learn about certain lesser-known dynamics of corporate existence that can provide your nonprofit with unforeseen corporate sponsorship opportunities.

One key to securing sponsorships is the ability to analyze what you are offering and how that stands up to what sponsors want. Just as we use past giving history to assess what an individual donor is capable of, in the case of sponsorship there are tools you can use to hone your sponsorship "ask" for greater success.

THE MATHEMATICS OF SPONSORSHIP

When considering proposals for a corporate sponsorship, marketers put emotions aside and resort to cold, logical reasoning. Sponsorship proposals are evaluated in accordance with a mathematical formula, as shown in Figure 11-1.

This is a mathematical formula that you as the fundraiser can use to evaluate your sponsorship proposals prior to submission. The point of the evaluation is to self-assess the likelihood that your proposal will be of interest to the corporation. The formula ($T \times I + G =$ Fair Market Value) outlines the basic metrics that corporations will use in their ratings.

Figure 11-1. Corporate calculator for sponsorship success.

$$T \times I + G = \text{Fair Market Value}$$

where:

T = tangible benefits

I = intangible benefits

G = geographic reach

T represents the sum of *tangible* benefits to the corporation (e.g., access to a nonprofit's membership, the use of the nonprofit's facilities for meetings and retreats, exposure in media friendly to the nonprofit). **I** is the sum of the *intangible* benefits (i.e., the prestige of the nonprofit, its track record for attracting coverage, its credibility). **G** simply stands for the *geographic* reach of the nonprofit. All of these factors are appraised in terms of dollars and cents. The Fair Market Value of the request—the resulting quantity—can be adjusted up or down by factors such as the supply of similar opportunities to connect with the nonprofit's constituency (positive) or a scandal enveloping the nonprofit (negative).

After a sponsorship engagement, another set of calculations is carried out to determine the actual outcomes of the deal. Surveys are conducted, and among the factors that are carefully measured are the extent to which consumers were aware of the partnership, shifts in consumer attitudes toward the brand, changes in sales patterns, the amount of buzz in social media, the impact of the partnership on employee morale, and changes in the value of the company's stock.

To interest sponsors in engaging with your organization, you have to explain what's in it for them. You must also demonstrate the passion your cause or organization inspires. Membership renewal rates and repeat visits to a nonprofit's program site or website are tangible measures of that passion. This is why I sometimes recommend that a nonprofit create a second, public-focused website to present information about its cause in a way that its primary website may not. The greater the public passion for the nonprofit's cause, the more value exists for the corporate sponsor because the sponsor is interested in changing the behavior of customers (i.e., increasing sales), and the key to changing behavior is to align with a source of emotional stimulation.

HOW CAN YOUR ORGANIZATION GET IN ON THIS CORPORATE LARGESSE?

Many corporations establish charitable institutions that function like private foundations and can be approached for small four- and five-figure donations the way you would approach any other grant maker. While most of the private foundations are located on the East and West Coasts, the Midwest has the largest number of corporate foundations, which is particularly good news for nonprofits located in the heartland. No matter where a foundation is located, the truly big money remains in the marketing activity known as sponsorship or "cause marketing."

At a corporate sponsorship panel I once attended, a JPMorgan Chase strategic philanthropy executive and two high-level consultants who had worked together on various projects described deals between the bank and the U.S. Open Tennis Championships. They discussed the recruitment of Pepsi-Cola, among other companies, as a sponsor for various causes, and eventually the floor was opened up for questions and answers. A long line formed behind the microphone. Almost everyone waiting to speak with the panelists represented a small or midsize nonprofit, and they all asked variations of the same question: How can we get in on this corporate largesse?

The panelists managed to entertain the question without truly answering it. One of the presenters went so far as to say, "Do anything to attract attention to your organization." One wonders what extremes she had in mind. *Have your agency staff march down Fifth Avenue in the nude?* The members of the panel certainly knew the answer to the question, but I suspect they couldn't bring themselves to speak it for fear of how this well-intentioned audience might respond. How could a high-level consultant bring herself to state the truth; namely, that small and midsize nonprofits (even those whose staff run naked down city thoroughfares) are almost entirely out of the running for a piece of the Great White Whale of fundraising: corporate sponsorships.

The reason these nonprofits get short shrift from corporate sponsors isn't complicated. There's no malice toward them or underlying disdain for what they do; it's simply a question of what marketers call "eyeballs." Corporations want to sell their products to millions of consumers. If a nonprofit organization can put the company's brand in front of large numbers of consumers (aka eyeballs), the company will get behind that organization and its cause. If not, it won't. This is because *sponsorship is not a philanthropic activity; it's a marketing proposition.* Companies routinely hire consultants who deploy sophisticated mathematical formulas (such as the one in Figure 11-1) to determine the amount of promotional bang they can expect for each buck devoted to a specified social cause.

Corporate sponsorships are meant to drive sales. The keywords in the vocabulary of corporate marketing executives concerning sponsorship are "reach" and "frequency." How many potential customers will be reached by identifying with a nonprofit and its cause, and how frequently will the company's brand be broadcast to the ears of those customers and displayed before their eyes?

Given these prerequisites, you might wonder how your agency, which is more than likely flying under the radar of most consumers, could ever hope to deliver enough "reach" and "frequency" to land a major corporate fish. To secure corporate sponsorships, a nonprofit has to *look* bigger as it works to get bigger. The nonprofit can project an image of being bigger than it is by association, which is to say, by forming strategic partnerships with other organizations. This can be done more rapidly and imaginatively than one might expect.

Case Study: Corporate Sponsorship for a National Organization

NAE Cohorts, a national nonprofit association of engineers, wanted to raise money for a workforce development program for American veterans of the Iraq and Afghanistan wars. The association held a golf tournament and a fundraising gala keyed to its annual convention, which was a major professional gathering for NAE's corner of the engineering universe. But neither of these events brought in the kind of money the association was looking for to serve a substantial number of veterans. However, the engineering group had a modest but ongoing relationship with an office of the U.S. Department of Defense (DOD) that utilized its services and supported its research studies. So I recommended that they try to nail down a partnership with the Department of Defense. The engineers and DOD had discussed partnering for a podcast that would inform servicemen and -women who were about to transition back into civilian life about the job opportunities in the specific field of engineering represented by NAE. That idea had fallen by the boards, though, because DOD was unable to find money in its budget to pay for it.

Nonetheless, this partnering idea served as the springboard for an eventual collaboration. NAE and DOD signed a Memorandum of Understanding for the purpose of finding a corporate sponsor to pay for the production of the podcast, as well as for associated flyers and brochures outlining the free training and employment assistance the engineering association made available to veterans. Since a corporate sponsor would have its brand on the podcast and print material, they could then offer a prospective sponsor the eyes and ears of every soldier, sailor, airman, and marine in the armed forces who was approaching retirement or separation from the service.

But that was just the tip of the promotional iceberg. NAE was planning to hold its next national conference in Salt Lake City, Utah, the capital of one of the five fastest-growing states in the country. The engineers realized that if they asked the commercial sponsor to also underwrite the cost of attendance of the first class of veterans benefiting from the program, they could offer the sponsor much more exposure. The plan called for the mayor of Salt Lake City to receive this class of veterans and, in an official ceremony at city hall, present a Best New Engineer of the Year Award, bestowed by the sponsor on the veteran demonstrating the most potential as a field engineer. Elected officials such as mayors, senators, and governors inevitably draw attention; the local media covers nearly every public activity they engage in. The local media in Salt Lake City reaches 3 million people.

The whole campaign was called Operation Infrastructure, because the engineering society was dedicated to increasing the number of engineers who worked on upgrading America's crumbling bridges and transportation systems. The promotional plan also called for the Salt Lake City Mayor's Office to declare "Operation Infrastructure Week" and to display banners with the sponsor's name and logo on all of the city's major roadways, which increased the sponsor's brand exposure yet again. Press releases highlighting the program, the award winner, and the sponsor's prominent role in the proceedings were sent to a number of additional markets selected in consultation with the sponsor. Local news media in the hometown of the Best New Engineer award winner were notified as well. In addition, the sponsor had a "boutique" at the conference that offered the 5,800 expected attendees an opportunity to view its products.

That's quite an attractive benefit package, especially from a group accustomed to flying under the radar. Tens of thousands of servicemen and -women every year, not to mention a sizable chunk of the adult population of a major U.S. city and a potential national readership, were added to a relatively small national organization of 20,000 members. And included in the cost of sponsorship, estimated at close to half a million dollars, was a budget line for the training and instruction of fifty veterans, NAE's most pressing need.

Case Study: Corporate Sponsorship for a Local Organization

A small youth development agency such as Forward Thinkers (FT) seemed an unlikely candidate for significant corporate sponsorship dollars since it only reached 1,000 children and families a year in New Orleans. But in looking around the city that FT served, it emerged that the economically challenged town had a number of things going for it. First, there was a public radio station broadcasting jazz and blues to listeners well beyond the boundaries of the city, which meant the potential "reach" of a promotional campaign was greater than it seemed. Second, there was a local symphony hall that produced concerts featuring a wide variety of music, including jazz and blues. This meant that a well-attended venue already existed to potentially host promotional opportunities. Third, the municipal government was headed by a popular, energetic, forward-looking mayor (read: headline-grabber).

These compelling elements were all combined into a half-million-dollar campaign blueprint for a jazz festival designed to net some $175,000 to be divided among the public radio station, the symphony hall, and Forward Thinkers. The campaign included:

- A series of five-minute radio spots to run on the radio station for a one-month period, each spot highlighting the career of a jazz musician who rose to prominence from the city or one of its surrounding communities

- A concert or series of concerts at the symphony hall, and possibly at additional outdoor locations
- An essay contest for high school students on the meaning of jazz in their town, with a college scholarship for the winner
- The development of a K–12 curriculum based on the city's jazz heritage
- Summer internships for up to four youths at the radio station and symphony hall, with stipends for travel and meals
- Temporary jobs for youths posting announcements of the events

Forward Thinkers would be the lead agency managing the engagement of youths with the campaign. FT's education director would be hired to review existing teaching material about jazz greats and develop a K–12 curriculum to be distributed electronically to the local superintendent of public schools and to after-school programs and youth organizations to improve literacy skills. The youths being served by FT would receive stipends for posting announcements of the concert(s) or selling tickets to the event(s), and they would be considered for internships wherever appropriate.

The radio station, symphony hall, and youth agency would form a committee to screen and review the essays and select a contest winner. The Office of the Mayor would be asked to officially declare a "Jazz Month" to coincide with the campaign. The mayor would present the lead sponsor's award at city hall for the essay contest and scholarship winner.

From the lead sponsor's vantage point, the benefit package now seemed very enticing. The company would have its brand:

- Identified on placards throughout the city and on banners on major arteries as the official sponsor of the jazz fest
- Identified as the official sponsor of the five-minute radio spots
- Exposed on large inflatable figures or objects associated with the company's products, which would be mounted outside of the symphony hall and other venues when the concerts were being staged
- Prominently displayed in newspaper ads for the concerts
- Uniquely positioned on the educational material distributed to schools and after-school programs
- Associated with the city hall ceremony honoring the winner of the essay contest and scholarship

Between all the events and the expected coverage in local media and on the Web, the total potential reach of the audience clocked in at an impressive 4.2 million people. The moral of this story is simple: Offer potential sponsors the eyes and ears of 4 million-plus residents of a major metropolitan market and they, too, will prick up their ears.

THE LITTLE-KNOWN DYNAMICS OF CORPORATE SPONSORS AND BOARD MEMBERS

In dealing with the corporate world, whether you are shooting for a modest grant or a sponsorship contract, it is instructive to consider certain lesser-known dynamics of both corporate board members and the companies they serve. There exists a sort of interlocking nature between corporate and nonprofit boards, by which I mean that influential people may sit on several different corporate boards as well as on the boards of several private foundations. I discovered this for myself while conducting research for a national nonprofit that was expert in public education. This agency produced many books and videos on various public education topics, all of them well done. Because of that treasure trove, I decided to approach large companies with an existing stake in public education for their sponsorship. My hunch was that someone sitting on the board of an education conglomerate would be value aligned enough to want to meet. That hunch was borne out by a flood of calls from board members with dual allegiances. Similar to the sort of revolving door that sometimes exists between the private sector and government (e.g., the military), the door between nonprofits and corporations will always stand a greater chance of opening if an alignment of values can be proffered from one to the other.

When it comes to sponsorship, there are many other factors at work as well. I had an in-depth conversation with a senior executive, whom I'll call George, who works on the corporate side of a very large philanthropy, evaluating proposals submitted by nonprofit organizations. For several years, he had been on the staff of one of the country's largest private insurers. "As soon as I went to work there," George said, "I started getting phone calls and e-mail from people who used their networks so well they had been able to get my contact information. They were well educated, wealthy, privileged people who attended Ivy League schools. They're much more forward and more confident than the average person, and they're not afraid to ask for the big dollars. They would say to me, 'This program strongly meets your guidelines. I need $75,000 to get it off the ground. Here's the breakdown.'"

Naturally, the lesson to draw from this anecdote isn't that you need to be rich and have an Ivy League degree to get sponsorships; rather, just like the small nonprofit in search of a larger audience reach, you have to project the same degree of confidence and have as well-thought-out a plan as the "big boys," which includes everyone seeking pieces of the sponsorship pie. As is the case with planned giving (which we'll look at in Chapter 13), active programs trump passive ones every time.

George also offered insight into why corporations often prefer to fund nonprofits based in areas near "company operations"—in other words, where the headquarters and manufacturing facilities are located—even though the company's products are sold all over the country.

"It helps politically," he explained. "Corporations have to maintain good relationships with senators from their home states and representatives from their home districts. The elected officials, in turn, want to see that the corporation is doing well for their constituents."

In addition, your nonprofit should also be aware that some business institutions are required to demonstrate to government regulators that they are in compliance with existing statutes. For instance, banks are examined every two years for compliance with the Community Reinvestment Act of 1977, legislation that was initially passed when redlining practices were common. "Regulatory compliance," said George, "means that if a bank, say, has taken deposits from a given community, it has to show that it is providing services to that community. This is why banks are often willing to sponsor affordable housing programs. Those kinds of sponsorships are taken into consideration by the regulators when the bank wants to open new branches or seeks approval for mergers and acquisitions."

Finally, George confirmed a notion alluded to at the outset of this chapter; namely, that corporations are stepping back from the $2,500 and $5,000 charitable handouts doled out by their foundation-giving arms in favor of more substantial and "meaningful" community investments. "It's all changing," he said. "Companies are becoming more strategic when it comes to philanthropy. That is, more focused, more thoughtful, more outcome-oriented. They want to know, 'What are we getting in return for this contribution? How is our money having an impact on social problems? Can it be measured?' And, of course, 'How can you help us increase awareness of our product and our brand?'"

These are the most salient forces you are up against when approaching corporations for sponsorship dollars. But as we've seen, if you can cleverly tap into your community's existing promotional resources, and if you are mindful of the exigencies of your corporate sponsor target, your nonprofit can share handsomely in the benefits of corporate sponsorship. You don't need a giant net to catch the Great White Sponsorship Whale. You just need the right bait.

AT THE END OF THE DAY

Corporate sponsorship is not a philanthropic activity; it's a marketing proposition. Your nonprofit's best bet for securing corporate sponsorship is to consider the following:

- Who are your natural corporate partners?
- What elements can you bring together to make your organization look bigger than it is?
- Which civic leaders and celebrities can you involve to generate press coverage?
- How can you increase "reach" and "frequency" for a potential corporate partner?
- What regulatory needs of the corporate partner can your nonprofit help fulfill?

CHAPTER TWELVE

Major Fundraising Campaigns: The Moral Equivalent of War

THE TIME HAS COME. YOU'VE thought about your culture, examined your leadership, tuned up your board, learned about challenge and stretch gifts, and built up your annual fund. The moment has arrived to put it all together into a major fundraising campaign. A major fundraising campaign is a period of sustained focus on a particular goal, during which you collect stretch gifts from current donors, usually through multiple year pledges, and bring in gifts from new donors who share your values and the campaign's goal. For our purposes, a major campaign is also the culmination of the ideas and tactics we've discussed so far.

The YMCA launched the first-ever campaign of this sort in the early years of the twentieth century.[1] Soon after, campaign firms were organized, with hospitals and colleges as their initial clients. Since those pioneering days, campaigns have become a standard practice for universities, hospitals, and other nonprofits that have natural constituencies (alumni, patients, and their families, among others) to turn to for major gifts.

The ability to organize a major campaign is a sign that your non-profit has a genuine plan to reach "the next level." It requires that you reflect on your own resources as well as on the board of directors, the staff, the volunteers, and the donors. This chapter is intended to guide you through those processes of reflection and planning in order to produce your own successful campaigns.

In this chapter, we'll look at:

- Why you should be thinking about a major fundraising campaign
- How to determine if you are ready
- What type of campaign is right for your agency
- How to prepare the campaign's case statement
- Campaign costs and how to cover them
- Securing capital through the issuance of bonds
- Donor engagement and naming opportunities
- Further preparation for a campaign
- The course of a campaign
- Why campaigns stall, fail, or succeed

Planning and executing a campaign is no walk in the park. A colleague of mine at Princeton, who for many years was the university's lead fundraiser, calls campaigns the moral equivalent of war. (Incidentally, the expression "moral equivalent of war" originally came from an eponymous 1910 speech by the psychologist William James.) Campaigns operate as an advanced form of fundraising and require a serious, fight-until-you-capture-the-flag mentality. But given the changing times that nonprofits are facing, major campaigns often make the difference between a future of survival and prosperity, as opposed to one of loss and stagnation.

WHY YOU SHOULD BE THINKING ABOUT A FUNDRAISING CAMPAIGN

When the social revolution of the 1960s led to more safety-net spending and government support for human services, smaller organizations began to question the need for campaigns and the pressure-cooker dynamics associated with them. Government came to be seen almost as a replacement revenue source, equally as lucrative as a fundraising campaign. But the facts of nonprofit life have changed in recent decades. Between 2001 and 2011, the number of nonprofits increased 25 percent; from 1,259,764 million to 1,574,674 million.[2] This rapid growth means increased competition for donor dollars. At the same time, the demand for services is also rising.

These twin phenomena pose serious challenges to the ability of nonprofit organizations to fulfill their missions. In 2011, the Nonprofit Research Collaborative (NRC) released a study concluding that increased demand for services and stagnant funding growth since late 2008 have generated urgent pressure to move forward with capital campaign planning throughout the nonprofit sector.[3]

Many organizations have put off their capital and special needs as long as possible. Organizations that undertake a campaign are more likely to increase donor revenue. Greater competition for limited funding sources is changing the fundraising strategies of many nonprofits, and more of them will be moving forward with capital campaigns in the next couple of years because they can't wait any longer. If you are not among them, you risk being left in the dust as compelling cases for contributions by other nonprofits are put before prospective donors. Clearly, then, it makes sense to be thinking about a capital campaign, though embarking on one can seem daunting, and for good reason.

ARE YOU READY FOR A CAMPAIGN?

The traditional answer to this question is that you're ready once you do a feasibility study and talk to twenty-five to fifty prospective donors to see if they would contribute to your fundraising campaign. A feasibility study (best done by an external, trained fundraising counsel) takes around three to five months and usually costs $25,000 to $45,000. The purpose of the feasibility study is to determine how your organization is viewed in the eyes of prospective donors, whether you have access to sufficient donor giving to reach your goal, and whether your community understands the importance of any proposed capital improvements with regard to the service that you propose. It's also an opportunity to engage prospective donors by inviting their input about your organization and the proposed campaign and, equally important, to assess your organizational infrastructure and its ability to handle all the particulars of a capital campaign.

If the findings demonstrate that your donors will give to the campaign, then your board can agree to proceed confidently to the so-called silent phase, in which you meet with donors until you secure 60 percent or more of your campaign goal. At that point you "go public" (i.e., beyond your initial donors) to raise the balance.

However, in my experience, the traditional answer is often incomplete because, for example, if your board is not an effective engine of fundraising, or if you lack a viable donor base, a strategic vision for the future, or a plan for staffing up to accommodate the needs of a campaign, you'd be better advised to define the steps required to get ready rather than waste time and money investigating what you already know won't suffice. Feasibility is important, but it can sometimes be supplanted by an *informal* (and free) process of self-study when first considering your campaign. You can meet with and get to know your donors, listen to what drives their interest in your agency (if anything), cultivate them, and increase their passion for your mission.

That's not to say there aren't valid reasons for engaging a third-party feasibility study. For one, donors often talk more candidly to professional fundraising counsel because their comments remain confidential. Also, a trained fundraiser can easily address technical questions that arise (say, about a planned or legacy gift) that someone less trained might not be able to answer. Lastly, feasibility determination takes time and requires a talented, dedicated project manager. However, too many agencies that are unable to afford the cost and the time of a traditional feasibility study mistakenly allow it to keep them from getting started. The bottom line is that *you should start where you are*, and *you shouldn't wait to begin*.

In the real world, defining the predevelopment steps to prepare for a campaign is the actual start of the campaign process. A successful campaign doesn't depend on following a strict set of rules designed for organizations with fully developed major donor programs; rather, as we'll see momentarily, it sinks or swims based on intangibles such as solid leadership, persistence in fundraising, and the ability to make the right adjustments midstream. Once you feel your organization is ready, based on your own feasibility assessment, you can segue to an objective third-party feasibility study or skip it entirely and proceed with the mechanics of your campaign. Both choices should be considered equally.

WHAT TYPE OF FUNDRAISING CAMPAIGN IS RIGHT FOR YOU?

There are a myriad of different fundraising campaigns, though the most prevalent are a capital campaign, an endowment campaign, a cash reserve campaign, a capacity-building campaign, and a comprehensive campaign. Let's review each.

- *Capital campaigns* raise money for a specific purpose, which could be to renovate an old building, erect a new one, build a new wing on an existing structure, or acquire some tangible asset such as a fleet of vans or gymnasium equipment.
- *Endowment campaigns* seek to increase the financial assets your agency has to invest so as to generate revenue for the organization without compromising its principal.
- *Cash reserve campaigns* solicit financial donations for an emergency fund, no larger than three times your annual budget. This fund is tapped for short-term needs, which saves you from having to dip into your long-term endowed investment capital.
- *Capacity-building campaigns* raise funds for specific infrastructure needs that improve the quality of your services (e.g., quality assurance, IT, human resources, administrative overhead, financial controls, planning services).
- *Comprehensive campaigns* can involve any or all of the aforementioned campaigns. A comprehensive campaign is an initiative to transform dedicated donors from patrons of your organization into full-fledged caretakers of your mission.

From a fundraiser's perspective, a donor has three financial roles. The first is as a contributor of annual gifts to meet your day-to-day organizational expenses. Donors are asked annually (or more frequently) for money and generally donate at a level commensurate with their earnings. The second role is as a potential "stretch giver." The nonprofit may ask the donor to give at an increased level "just this one time," for a capital or cash reserve campaign, for instance, and that gift may be in the form of a pledge over multiple years. The third role, in the donor's "sunset years," is as a planned or legacy giver.

The comprehensive campaign looks at donors in each of these three roles simultaneously, and attempts to broaden the donor's perception to the overall needs of the organization. In a comprehensive campaign, the fundraiser seeks to move the donor to multiple, simultaneous levels of giving, as shown in the pyramid of giving (see Figure 12-1). The beauty of a comprehensive campaign is that it prevents the fundraiser and the organization from wearing out their welcome by asking donors for too many gifts on too many occasions. An overall plan is developed in accordance with each donor's interests and needs. Participation in this type of campaign is the surest statement of a relationship based on the shared values of the donor and your organization.

The pyramid of giving allows you to see how campaigning builds on the basics of fundraising and how all aspects of fundraising come together in a campaign, especially when the campaign is of a comprehensive nature. If you build an effective donor base, develop effective leadership, energize the board, and establish a functional leadership council, your campaign will blaze forward and meet all of its goals.

PREPARING THE CASE STATEMENT

Your campaign and the reasons to support it become truly manifest with your preparation of a document known as a case statement. The case statement expresses what the problem is, why it needs to be addressed now, who will lead the effort, and how the problem

Figure 12-1. The Pyramid of Giving.

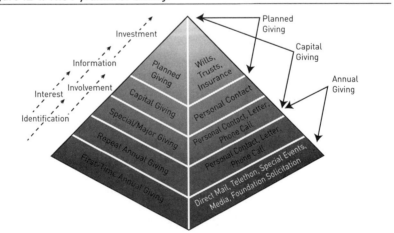

will be remedied as a result. It literally "makes the case" for the campaign. But the object of the case statement isn't just to present an argument for the campaign. Its purpose is to move the donor to action. A good case statement will make the donor say, upon reaching the conclusion of the document, "Sign me up." It is therefore an overture and a bugle call, both an appeal to reason and a call to action, part Thomas Jefferson and part Thomas Paine.

If you have existing strategic plans, business plans, or program plans, you can draw on these documents to create the campaign's case for support. But the case statement is not the same as any of these plans. It should succinctly lay out the story of the organization and the need it is seeking to address. It should describe how much money has to be raised and how the funds will be spent. It should map out the leadership structure for the campaign, including the cabinet. And it should give the prospective donor a sense of where the campaign currently stands: "This is how much we've raised so far; this is what we have to raise now."

How much detail should you provide? Enough to make donors feel that all the bases have been covered, that you know what you're doing, and that you are proceeding in a rational way. In some cases it makes sense to create both a long and a short version of your case statement. The short one of approximately four or five pages is for the type of donor who prefers an "executive summary." The longer version, which is twelve to fifteen pages, is for those who make the largest gifts, such as a foundation or individuals of the highest net worth; these donors may undertake a broader review and would want specific technical information, such as dimensions of the physical plant (in a capital campaign), how capacity needs were determined (in a capacity campaign), and what metrics support your assumptions about why you need the money (for any type of campaign).

You don't have to overstate your case to persuade potential donors to support your organization. Just tell the story simply, movingly, clearly, and factually, and demonstrate that the organization has done its homework. An excellent example of a case statement is available online at www.thenonprofitfundraisingsolution.com

Before giving your case statement to the donor, you will need to get the board's approval on the assumptions behind it. A word of caution, though: Don't involve the board as a whole in *writing* the statement. Artful documents do not come from committees. One writer should be designated to draft the case statement, with comments solicited draft by draft. In this way, members can comment without slowing down the drafting process itself.

CAMPAIGN COSTS AND HOW TO COVER THEM

The cost of a campaign represents a significant investment for any organization. The industry standard for capital campaign expenses (including external consultants, in-house organizational staff, design and printing of campaign materials, other personnel services, and overhead) is roughly 20 percent to 30 percent of the campaign goal. Campaigns are often more expensive the first time out, usually by 5 percent to 10 percent, due to inexperience, prolonged feasibility studies, and because materials and templates are being created for the first time, just to name a few reasons. I strongly recommend you fold the costs related to running your campaign into the campaign's overall goal. This simple move obviates overspending, and creates a literal win-win as revenues accrue.

Institutions that campaign at least twice a decade are more robust and better able to fulfill their missions. You can create a culture of campaigning using one campaign as a springboard to the next. For example, one nonprofit I worked with ran its first-ever campaign—a capital campaign—and then immediately began a campaign for government matching funds as soon as the first one ended, all within thirty months. Perhaps your endowment needs are pressing at the same time that a large transfer of wealth is occurring in planned gifts. By cultivating a culture open to campaigning, you won't miss out on opportunities due to a lack of preparedness. The benefit of campaigning should be an enduring culture of giving. This is the ultimate value for any nonprofit organization.

While every responsible organization wants to preserve its resources when possible, being aggressively thrifty in a campaign can seriously undermine the effort. Spending less on the staffing of a campaign, for example, often compromises your ability to attain your goal. As the saying goes, you mustn't trip over quarters to pick up pennies. Instead, avail yourselves of existing strategies to mitigate costs and keep your focus on your overall fundraising goals.

Five Suggestions for Covering Campaign Costs

For those nonprofits that have the need and the desire to launch a campaign, but lack the funds to do so, here are five suggestions for paying the underlying costs of a campaign:

1. Seek out a supportive major donor, share the written campaign plans, and ask this one donor to underwrite one year of the campaign work. Similarly, you can approach the board for a collective stretch gift dedicated to financing the effort.

2. Apply for foundation capacity-building grants, where you share the proposed plan and ask a foundation to underwrite it. Research must be done up front to make sure the foundation welcomes such proposals.

3. Host a onetime special event—or dedicate the funds from an upcoming event—to raise the campaign costs, with a goal of raising enough for one year's work.

4. If other noncampaign resources are available, redirect them in support of a campaign. One agency I worked with dedicated two planned gifts it received to pay for the costs of a campaign. Another sold a piece of property that had long been out of use.

5. Redirect the funds that you budgeted for other development staff to offset campaign costs. This last tactic can be tricky because you don't want to fix one thing and harm another, so be judicious.

No matter which route(s) you choose, never borrow against the agency's credit card or line of credit to pay for a campaign. It can lead to disaster.

SECURING CAPITAL THROUGH BONDS

Yet another efficient process for raising campaign capital is to work with a third party to issue tax-free bonds. Many states have agencies whose activities include making financial resources available to nonprofits through bond financing and loan guarantee programs. Agencies such as the Dormitory Authority of the State of New York and the New Jersey Economic Development Authority, to name just two, can be instrumental in taking you to your campaign goal.

Or, on a national level, there's the Nonprofit Finance Fund (whose slogan is, "Where Money Meets Mission").

One nonprofit in New York that was looking to build and administer housing for its clients determined through a feasibility study that it only had the capacity to raise $600,000 of a $6 million goal—a shortfall of $5.4 million. Clearly in need of an alternative path, the nonprofit managed to persuade the city of New York to donate the building in which its program was instituted while the Dormitory Authority of the State of New York issued municipal bonds to meet the remainder of the other financial needs. The building now provides apartments to the poor and otherwise homeless.

How can such an approach work for you? When attempting to secure bond financing, your agency might reach out to a local law firm that deals or specializes in nonprofits and ask if the firm does bond syndication (i.e., bond financing). Although you are borrowing money, either from the bond market or from the government, remember that some of the monthly service costs on the bonds can be mitigated through fee-for services you charge or, in the case of housing, through Section 8 vouchers that the client brings. In an era of low interest rates, such as the time of this writing, bond financing is an especially worthwhile avenue to explore.

NAMING OPPORTUNITIES AS A REVENUE STRATEGY

Capital campaigns frequently offer naming opportunities to donors. These programs acknowledge significant givers by creating plaques or naming buildings, wings, or rooms in their honor. The revenues from this strategy can be significant. But there is another, more profound reason for naming honors. They add a special dimension to the relationship between an organization and its supporters. The personal story of the donor can be made part of the spirit of your mission, which is a perfect example of value-aligned giving.

LEADERSHIP STRUCTURE IN A MAJOR CAMPAIGN

The leadership of a campaign is usually carried out by a campaign cabinet of twelve to twenty people drawn from your agency and the community at large. The cabinet is responsible for the critical tasks of overseeing the entire campaign and establishing its goals and tone. Some campaigns break the full cabinet into subcommittees to handle much of the campaign detail work. The subcommittees can be delineated as, say, corporations, government relations, banking bridge loans, major donors, religious congregations, speakers' bureaus, and special events. The full committee should meet every two or three months for the duration of the campaign; the subcommittees should meet as appropriate, usually weekly, although it's important to set a regular published schedule of meetings so that attendance remains high. Since this is an awful lot to manage, it really pays to keep the cabinet and meeting structures simple.

The cabinet is there to bring in wealth for the campaign and to make sure the fundraising efforts are being conducted proactively. You can think of your cabinet almost as a "board" for your campaign.

In deciding who should sit on these committees, several factors come into play. Management and leadership skills can contribute a lot to a campaign cabinet; so, too, can individuals of high net worth who can make a lead gift themselves and secure lead gifts from their friends, family, work colleagues, and business and community networks. Special consideration should be given to deciding who should chair or cochair the cabinet. This decision is usually based on the individual's community position and ability to access a personal network to support the campaign in real dollars. It's usually not someone who is currently a board or staff member; rather, you want people who can make the campaign their top priority, address community gatherings on your behalf (i.e., serve as a "point person" for the campaign), and solicit significant contributions from colleagues, family, and friends. If you don't vet and appoint cabinet members properly, you risk wasting time with the wrong chairperson(s) and stalling the campaign, if not actually killing it.

Strategies to identify prospective leaders and the right volunteers can be built into your feasibility process, and a defined "talent search" plan can be created to state how you intend to find them. First, you are looking for people who can make lead gifts at least in the top 50 percent of your gift chart (you can easily create a gift chart by inputting your fundraising target at www.giftrangecalculator. com). Second, you want people who can access their own network and wrangle community members who will respond to them asking for donations. Third, you'll need people with business sensibilities to monitor the campaign's progress and take corrective action when necessary. Finally, you need people who are inspiring and can truly sell why the campaign is so absolutely necessary.

While these strategies are similar to the process I discussed for choosing a leadership council in Chapter 10, remember that a leadership council does "light lifting." A major campaign is heavy lifting. You mustn't feel compelled to take any warm body that comes your way. Set criteria for what you are looking for and stick with them.

THE SPECIAL ROLE OF YOUR BOARD IN THE CAMPAIGN

While your board carries out its normal functions during a major campaign, it has four additional responsibilities. It must vet and approve the feasibility study (or in the case of a capital campaign, any engineering feasibility reports on structures to be built). It must then authorize the campaign. It must also, if it hasn't already done so, create gift acceptance policies (discussed in Chapter 3) to address the types of gifts the campaign may receive (e.g., stocks, real estate).

Finally, and most important, all board members must be solicited for a stretch gift—that is, a gift beyond their annual giving designated for the campaign. This is crucial because your case statement will need to say that you have 100 percent board giving; otherwise, it will not be clear whether your board is game for the rigors of campaigning and you'll handicap the campaign's future giving from others. If board members won't commit their own philanthropy now, they surely won't be able to convincingly ask others to give later. When board members lead the way in making a campaign gift, they are saying to others "Join me!" If they can't say that, they shouldn't be on your board in the first place.

FURTHER PREPARATION FOR THE CAMPAIGN

Here are some other actions that will benefit your planning:
- Consider establishing a leadership council (as discussed in Chapter 10) prior to the campaign to help you elevate the profile of your organization.

- If you haven't already done so, move your donor database online to make it accessible to campaign staff members and volunteers. You can make use of existing resources, such as techsoup.org.
- Determine in advance what you need the money for and if the goal you have in mind is adequate. In many cases, the money that nonprofit organizations project as campaign goals is less than what they really need.
- Draft a community communications plan to raise the profile of your agency before the campaign starts. This plan can include items such as the campaign's advertising budget, press releases, and op-ed strategies.[4]
- Develop a campaign budget to determine if the revenue goal you have in mind is, in fact, the right size. The first projection of the campaign goal is frequently less than what the organization really needs, and many organizations forget to fold the costs related to running the campaign into the goal. The budget should include a narrative that explains how the numbers were crafted and determined.
- Revise your case statement as necessary.
- Adjust and augment your routine communications with donors to ensure that your annual fund is strong and not at risk of being cannibalized by the campaign.
- Boost your relations with existing donors by meeting with the top 20 percent of givers to learn more about them and to give them a personal update about your agency.

How long should readiness preparation last? Some prep periods are as short as six months; others might last a few years. Every organization is unique. The simplest answer is that it will take as long as it needs to.

THE COURSE OF THE CAMPAIGN

Although campaigns are different, there are essentially six phases to each. The first two phases encompass everything we've discussed thus far in this chapter. The remaining four phases, linked to the actual fundraising goals, occur while the campaign is fully under way.

Phase 1: Preparation

Phase 2: Planning

Phase 3: Leadership gifts (by the end of which you've raised 20 percent to 40 percent of your goal)

Phase 4: Advance gifts (by the end of which you've raised 40 percent to 60 percent of your goal)

Phase 5: Public outreach (by the end of which you've raised 100 percent of your goal)

Phase 6: Celebration, pledge collection monitoring, donor cultivation, and ongoing development plan definition

Once your campaign is under way, there are several benchmarks to reach, as well as a number of ongoing tasks to adhere to. Here's a sample listing of the targets you'll be aiming for (although they may vary, according to your campaign's day-to-day and long-term needs):

- Campaign cabinet formed
- Leadership gifts from campaign cabinet members secured
- Kickoff/announcement made in the presence of the media (once 60 percent of the goal is secured)
- Additional leadership (including at least one major "pacesetter") committed
- Quarterly progress reports (phases 3 and 4) or monthly progress reports (phase 5) completed
- Ongoing meetings with major prospects for cultivation and solicitation conducted
- Ongoing publicity for and announcements of major gifts received/pledged
- Ongoing promotion in all media, especially social media
- End-of-campaign celebration when 100 percent of goal secured (phase 6)
- Dedication of new facility and/or commemorative plaques

Figure 12-2 provides a breakdown of campaign tasks by phase. Major campaigns require a no-holds-barred attitude, in which all of your fundraising tactics are brought to bear. Since all campaigns are different, there is not one set way to run them, though they all share certain common elements. For instance, all campaigns should think through what announcements go through the media and when, in line with your communications plan. In most cases, once the lead gifts are secured, an announcement will also be made for a kickoff event, which can be anything from a prayer gathering, to a donor's luncheon, to a 10K run, to a symphony performance at the local music conservatory. The most important consideration is how effectively the kickoff event will promote your campaign to those you seek to reach.

As you'll see in Figure 12-2, there are many variables to each campaign. Your campaign could be a good time to ask volunteers and board members to reach out to family members for "family" gifts. Some of your major donors might be best approached with a short, three-page proposal that targets them more specifically than through the case statement alone. During the "advanced gifts" stage, you will probably want to differentiate and develop solicitation strategies by categories, such as foundations, families, and large and small givers.

As with every major fundraising endeavor, supporting the staff and volunteers throughout all phases of the campaign is a sound practice and should not be overlooked. Conduct training sessions with your volunteers and your board, and coach them about how to ask for support. This work will keep your campaigns driving forward instead of petering out.

WHY CAMPAIGNS STALL, FAIL, OR SUCCEED

While proper training is a vital component of campaign success, the main reason most campaigns stall or fail outright is more structural in nature: The organization finds it doesn't have enough donors or members to solicit. There simply aren't enough donors and prospective donors in the pipeline. You can prevent this situation from happening by choosing campaign cabinet members who have strong networks; otherwise, you have to go back to fundraising basics and create a donor base where none exists.

You must also expand the human talent available to your organization and invite new community leaders to join your efforts. Your campaign's success depends on your choosing a volunteer structure that is uniquely suited to your organization and your community, and that will effectively accomplish your campaign goals. These volunteers can't just be anyone who is available. You need experienced

Figure 12-2. Phases of a capital campaign.

Preparation	Planning	Leadership Gifts	Advance Gifts	Public Phase	Cleanup and Celebration
• Clarify mission and vision • Define need for a campaign • Strengthen board • Cultivate donors and volunteers • Strengthen staff • Select consultants • Develop prospect lists • Initiate campaign cost-mitigation steps • Initiate tax-free bond discussions • Move donor database online • Draft budget • Draft communications plan	• Establish campaign cabinet • Create leadership councils • Conduct feasibility study • Assemble steering committee • Draft case statement • Outline timetable • Establish gift acceptance policies • Determine financial goal • Identify leadership • Establish subcommittees • Review gift chart • Identify and enlist volunteers for soliciting lead gifts • Identify naming opportunities	• Review prospect list for leadership gifts • Evaluate prospects • Develop solicitation strategy for each gift • Prepare three-page targeted major donor proposals • Conduct major donor meetings • Train volunteers • Solicit gifts • Identify and enlist volunteers for soliciting gifts	• Review prospect list for "family" gifts • Evaluate prospects • Develop solicitation strategy for each category of prospects • Train volunteers • Prepare proposals • Solicit gifts • Identify and enlist volunteers for general public phase	• Review prospect list for public phase • Prepare targeted letter to top 20 percent of remaining donors to solicit stretch gifts • Train volunteers • Kick off campaign • Solicit gifts • Hold a phone-a-thon • Execute a direct mail campaign	• Do a solicitation follow-up • Report results to campaign volunteers • Acknowledge volunteers • Extend extra thanks to donors • Reinforce relationship with volunteers and donors

Subcommittees

Building
Public Relations
Finance
Prospect Cultivation
Hospitality/Events

Optional Celebrations

Campaign kickoff
Goal-reaching party
Groundbreaking
Open house

senior community leaders and philanthropists. You may have to look beyond the leaders within your organization to the community at large to recruit a sufficient level and quantity of talent, but it is well worth it to do so in the long run. It will take time, it will be difficult, and you can expect to hear a lot of "No thanks," but the right combination of two or three leaders is often all you need.

I'm often asked what keeps a campaign from falling flat on its face. My first answer is always "leadership, leadership, leadership." Solid leadership keeps energy and emotions high so that a sense of urgency is present throughout the campaign structure. Urgency is important both to honor the project's values and for a vital business reason: The longer you take to complete the campaign, the more expensive it becomes. However, just because you set a goal of three years (the average length of time a campaign usually takes) doesn't mean you have to take all thirty-six months. Why not wrap it up in a year and apply the savings to your next development effort or even your next campaign? Strong leadership can accelerate a campaign as well as guide it to its goals.

Leadership in the context of a major campaign also requires conducting business-oriented reviews along the way. These are "big picture" reviews to analyze the campaign's ROI in terms of time, energy, processes, and funds raised vs. funds expended, as well as to assess the campaign's level of engagement with its community. It probably goes without saying that the point of a review is to take corrective action and to reinforce your strengths. Otherwise, why bother? Here again, good leadership recognizes and accepts mistakes and continually seeks to improve on past performance.

—————— ☙ CASEBOOK ☙ ——————

Here's an example of a nontraditional approach that got a faltering campaign unstuck. I was providing counsel for a suburban library that was roughly equidistant from two towns. Most of the library's members came from Town A, but Town B, which also used the library, happened to be where the money was. But the high net worth individuals living in Town B were not committed to the library or to its cause, and the library couldn't generate enough revenue through its campaign cabinet.

To remedy this situation, we purchased and wealth-vetted a mailing list of 2,000 households in Town B (for a cost of $300), knowing that each person on the list earned more than $120,000 a year and had a history of making charitable contributions elsewhere. Rather than add these names to our mailing list from the get-go, we instead asked ourselves who might know these 2,000 prospective donors and soon figured out the obvious: the mayor of Town B. We began discussions with the mayor and eventually recruited her as a member of our campaign cabinet. We explained our need to organize an event in Town B so that we could make a pitch for the library and collect as many people as possible for our mailing list. The mayor became our linchpin, calling upon a local top-tier restaurant to donate its facilities free of charge.

We invited 220 of our best prospects to a "party with a purpose" and raised $100,000 after expenses. Not only did we revitalize our campaign with a fresh infusion of cash, we brought in the promise of future giving from the new donors we could now begin cultivating. Even the mayor joined the library's board.

AT THE END OF THE DAY

The late Malcolm Forbes, former publisher of *Forbes Magazine*, once said, "Diamonds are nothing more than chunks of coal who stuck to their jobs." In the context of a difficult major campaign, that sentiment can be downright inspiring. Solid leadership, persistence, and careful donor cultivation will always carry the day. Feasibility studies have their place as well, but they shouldn't be relied upon to entirely define your agency's campaign readiness or probability of success, nor should they be an excuse to delay starting the work. Start from where you are, and work your way forward. Otherwise, your donors may contribute elsewhere.

Chapter Thirteen

Creating or Advancing Your Planned Giving Program

Most people spend forty years building their wealth, ten years protecting it, and only two hours determining its disposition through their estate plans, if at all. Not only is this a remarkable disparity of attention, it also illustrates why planned giving programs are often nonexistent or languishing inertly at most nonprofits. Yet ironically, especially given its common (though sometimes inaccurate) association with life's end, planned giving is often the most rewarding aspect of a philanthropist's engagement with a favorite charity. And for charities, planned gifts are far and away the most lucrative. It is estimated that between $6 trillion and $11.6 trillion in charitable bequests will be made between 1998 and 2052 alone (unadjusted for inflation).[1]

Woody Allen once joked, "I'm not afraid of death; I just don't want to be there when it happens." While it's true that most people shy away from end-of-life discussions, those same people are generally willing to express through their last will and testament what they want to happen once they've moved on from their terrestrial existence, especially those with material assets to bequeath. By some estimates, only 50 percent of Americans leave a will, yet principal among these are high net worth individuals, the vast majority of whom see to their wills with, if you'll forgive the expression, a vengeance. Whether or not planned *giving* is being done in conjunction with your nonprofit, there is an immeasurable amount of *planning* going on among your donors that you can and ought to be a part of.

Consider the real story of Victor and his wife, Linda, who had been faithful donors to several organizations in their community for thirty-five years. Victor gave most significantly to a local private secondary school that he helped found more than twenty years ago. Every year he wrote a check to the school, and during the past four years, his annual gift was $7,500.

One day, the school's headmaster received word that Victor had passed away. Not long after, he received a letter from Victor's attorney informing him that the school would receive a bequest of $30,000 from Victor's estate. At first, the headmaster was pleased to see that Victor had left a legacy that was four times as large as any gift he had made in the past. However, the headmaster quickly realized that he had probably missed a significantly larger opportunity. A bit of further research uncovered that Victor was one of the wealthiest men in town.

Victor and Linda had each prepared simple wills that essentially left everything to each other, with some provisions for their favorite individual charities. Since Linda was the primary beneficiary of Victor's will, all of his wealth would be transferred to her, with the exception of three bequests of $30,000 each. Victor's legacy to the school was only four years' value of his former gift. After that, his contribution wasn't continued because Linda had different interests. The headmaster realized that the school that Victor had helped to found, and to which he dedicated much of his time on earth, had lost an important donor. The deeper lesson he learned was this: There's no deep psychoanthropological reason to explain why people give in life and don't give in death; it's purely tactical. People will give, but somebody needs to ask them to.

In this chapter we'll look at:
- How to create and market your planned giving program
- How to address and overcome donor resistance to planned giving
- How to mitigate the costs of your program
- When to consider donor-advised funds and legacy societies

Planned giving is a market-oriented approach to fundraising, steeped in a mutually beneficial arrangement between donors and their nonprofit of choice. Donors reduce their taxes, satisfy other personal financial needs, and/or create a legacy. The nonprofit receives a significant gift. By pursuing a planned giving program, nonprofits can deepen their relationship with their donors while capitalizing on the opportunities presented by America's blossoming rate of wealth transfer, estimated to reach more than $40 trillion over the next four decades.[2]

Unlike gifts to a capital campaign, planned gifts are typically made when the donor is ready and when the time and gift vehicle (e.g., a gift in trust, a bequest, a gift of real estate) fit the individual donor's circumstances and need. However, just like capital campaigns, the donor needs to be properly informed and actively encouraged to participate.

HOW TO CREATE YOUR PLANNED GIVING PROGRAM

The responsibility to educate donors about planned giving falls squarely on your shoulders. Unfortunately, most nonprofits allot planned giving about as much time as donors allocate to it; meaning, almost no time at all. Hesitancy around planned giving typically comes from a self-generated perception by smaller organizations that they are "too overwhelmed" to focus on it and lack the requisite people power or financial resources to make planned giving a part of their overall development program.

We know that in the course of a person's lifetime about 65.5 percent of Americans give a gift to charity,[3] but only 4.6 percent of all decedents over age 55 leave a charitable bequest.[4] Even more troubling, 38.2 percent of Americans over age 50 who have put estate planning documents in place do not include giving to charity. The implications of these statistics are clear: If the nonprofit doesn't ask for a bequest or a gift, it's virtually certain it won't get one. Most people assume donors don't give to charities in their wills because they want all the money to go to their families. Nothing could be further from the truth. Time and again, as organizations begin planned giving programs, dozens of people sign up right away when they see how simple it is. That number of participants increases even more as more people digest the inherent tax efficiencies that planned giving offers.

For donors, becoming a planned giver is sometimes as simple as inserting a sentence in their will that reads, roughly, "Upon my death, with the proceeds that are left after my expenses are paid, I'd like to give 5 percent or $5,000, whichever is larger, to XYZ charity." There's no great mystery to it. One wonders why planned giving is perceived as being so much more complex. Perhaps it's because it often involves attorneys and accountants (though, by that line of thinking, dare I say, country club membership is even more complex). I often suggest that donors speak with a financial adviser trained in planned giving to learn about their many giving options, as this professional can help to clarify a number of issues and reveal why planned gifts may be a good avenue for them.

Passive Marketing Strategies Are Usually Not Enough

Some agencies use passive marketing tools that they believe to be adequate, such as a planned giving brochure with a link on their website to that same brochure. If they are extremely lucky, these tools alone can be sufficient, but that's rarely the case. I once sent a planned giving brochure to a single man in Florida. The pamphlet mentioned that he could donate his house to a particular charity (a cultural museum) upon his death and that the house would, in turn, be sold by the charity according to its gift acceptance policy (yet another reason it is imperative for nonprofits to have these policies in place). The agency's policy was to immediately sell any donated houses or stocks because it didn't want to be in the housing or investment business; it just wanted to run its programs. The man ended up calling us and said, "You solved a huge problem for me. I didn't know *what* to do with my house. No one else in my family needs it after me. I was really stuck and wanted something good to happen with it. I love this charity, I want to leave the house to them—and by the way, it's good for me from a tax perspective."

While this gentleman's response was not atypical of planned givers, the fact that he responded to a lone brochure was a true anomaly. Larger nonprofits such as universities, hospitals, and national organizations know that passive programs usually yield pitiable results, if any. That's why they implement sophisticated systems of educating their donors and procuring planned gifts. Unfortunately, in spite of its enormous upside potential, relatively few smaller non-profits make an active effort to treat planned giving with the same respect as other development activities.

Admittedly, there is a demarcation between when a passive planned giving program is satisfactory and when a more assertive approach is necessary. Fundraisers often diverge on how best to determine that threshold. Some fundraisers contend you need at least 400 active donors, age 55 and over, to justify the expenses of marketing an active program. Others say it should be 40 percent of your over-55 active donor list, no matter how small the list. But research data indicates that as much as 40 percent of people aged 40–49 say they will probably or definitely make a planned gift in the future.[5] Clearly, the age of your prospects should not be the principal determinant in whether or not you will actively market planned giving. Instead, you can use a higher-level approach in which, rather than asking if your donors are old enough, you ask whether they are old enough to plan for the future.

Given these uncertainties, it makes sense to assess the size of your donor market so that you can match your marketing approach accordingly. Consider testing the waters with these questions, which you can insert into your annual donor survey:

- Are we included in your estate plans (i.e., last will and testament)?
- If we are not included, would you consider naming us in your will? If you say yes, we will mail you information about our tax-deductible planned giving options.

Small and midsize nonprofits that have developed individual donor bases and wish to reach a higher level of fundraising success will inevitably need to get up to speed and establish active planned giving strategies as a central part of their development function. If they don't, not only might they have no guarantee of a long-term future, they can be certain of having walked away from copious, often game-changing revenue.

Active Strategies Deliver Superior Results

Given the singular kind of lucrative payoff that a planned giving program portends, it should be compulsory for every nonprofit to make a careful tally of resources and determine if a few hours a week by one trusted individual couldn't be somehow allocated toward advancing a planned giving development strategy. Failing that, outsourcing is an option worth considering as well.

The same is true of any of the more knowledge-intensive components of planned giving. There are countless tax experts (aka accountants and financial advisers) who can help you should the need arise, and most of your larger donors will already have their own tax consultants; you needn't reinvent the tax wheel yourself to engage with them.

The key to a successful planned giving program is communication. It's important to utilize a wide array of tactics to systematically convey the planned giving message to donors, emphasizing the importance of estate planning and the tax benefits associated with having a good plan in place. Contact and communicate with your planned giving prospects as you normally would. Schedule a meeting to talk specifically about planned giving or bring it up in one of your regular meetings. However you usually communicate with these donors, by e-mail or regular mail, use those same channels to initiate your discussion.

As part of a comprehensive planned giving marketing strategy, two distinct marketing approaches are best applied. The first type is targeted marketing aimed at your most committed longtime supporters. To identify them, begin by examining each donor's giving history, paying particular attention to the donor's level of giving over an extended period of time. Based on your ability to extract this information from your database, you can tailor your selection process and concentrate your planned giving marketing on a special targeted group. Your final list is likely to feature loyal, committed donors and board members. What you are looking for is evidence of consistent support, be it financial or otherwise. For example, you'll want to include volunteers who perhaps don't give much money but who regularly give you their time or engage with your agency in other ways. Demonstrated loyalty is the most accurate predictor of prospective planned giving.

Central to targeted marketing is telling donor stories. Such stories motivate others to give and generate repeat giving among existing donors. The emotional impact of a heartfelt story of a donor who was able to make a significant gift without adversely affecting his or her finances (and who received tax benefits, to boot) can be magical. A real-life story illustrates the effectiveness of planned giving in ways that technical gift details never can. I prefer stories that are real, although composite stories are a reasonable substitute when necessary.

Target marketing usually includes mailings or events. For mailings, I highly recommend using large postcards (8.5" × 6") instead of long, tedious newsletters. My experience is that postcards get read. Sending three or four planned giving postcards every year, from February through May, plus one additional card in the month of September, is generally most effective.

The second marketing approach, known as broadcast marketing, is instead aimed at all of your donors. Broadcast marketing includes tactics such as planned giving web pages, receipt stuffers, newsletter articles, or a simple "Please remember us in your will" as part of your e-mail signature. These items are easy to administer and are important aspects of a planned giving program because they create awareness among all of your donors. This awareness will make your targeted group more likely to respond positively to the appeals they receive. In addition, broadcast marketing will typically generate its own steady flow of interested individuals outside your target groups. Broadcast marketing is an excellent means of communicating tax-advantaged current giving and gift annuity opportunities to your donors.

Target and broadcast marketing tactics are both important and complement each other well in maximizing the overall effectiveness of your planned giving program.

Whichever approach you ultimately choose, be proactive and take concrete steps. You can even start by offering one or two educational seminars to donors about the mutual benefits of planned giving. The truth is that with planned giving, time is of the essence. Many fundraisers don't realize that the average time from when a gift is planned to when it is distributed at the end of the donor's life is seven to ten years.

DEALING WITH DONOR RESISTANCE

As mentioned at the outset of this chapter, planned giving taps into some sensitive areas of human nature and mortality. Even when presented with all the right facts, some donors may still resist planned giving, insisting that they only want to make bequests to surviving spouses, children, and grandchildren. Others express concerns about outliving their resources, especially as people live longer. Still others are unable to visualize the legacy of their lifelong efforts or to feel confidence that their wishes will be faithfully fulfilled once they are gone. These are real and well-founded objections that nonprofits can overcome, but only if they consciously and conscientiously address them with donors.

One excellent option is to offer both restricted (e.g., development funding only or capital improvements only) and unrestricted planned gifts, thereby enabling donors to select a specific area of interest to support in the long term. With this option, donors can pick an area that meets their charitable interests while helping to sustain a particular program, service, or facility need in the future. Another creative strategy is to suggest donors make a two-pronged contribution in which a portion of the gift is designated for current use while the balance is earmarked as a planned gift. This way, donors can see an impact today while also building confidence that in the longer term, their gift will make a difference for the constituencies of tomorrow.

Curiously, many organizations fall prey to the false notion that the overall "pie" of donations is limited, and if you allow annual fund donors to be solicited for planned gifts, it will decrease the amount of dollars for the annual fund. Just the opposite is true. A 2007 study by the Center on Philanthropy at Indiana University found that when you approach donors loyal to your mission and they make a long-term commitment through a planned gift, they actually increase the size of their annual donation because they have furthered their investment in your mission. The study also revealed that annual gifts by legacy donors were twice the size of those of nonlegacy donors. By looking out for the donors' best interest and what they want to accomplish for your agency, you actually increase the size of the pie and your piece of it.[6] Figure 13-1 illustrates the three distinct ways your donors help to meet your organization's needs over the course of their lives.

COST VERSUS ROI OF PLANNED GIVING

As with any development strategy, cost is always a paramount concern. The cost of developing a solid planned giving program is far

Figure 13-1. Three aspects of giving over a donor's life span.

Overall, we are asking our donors to think of us in three ways in order to match our organizational need to the donor's income sources.

ORGANIZATION'S NEEDS	DONOR HELPS BY USING
1. Annual expenses	Yearly income
2. Capital	Assets (savings, property, stocks)
3. Endowment	Estate

outweighed by its benefits. In the absence of formal research, some informal research indicates costs ranging as low as 4 cents to 10 cents per dollar raised. Still, no matter how well your planned giving program is implemented, the program should be seen as an investment of today's dollars for tomorrow's benefits. The only way to shorten this time disparity is by targeting planned giving toward older, committed supporters with long giving histories.

Another good option to mitigate these initial costs is to seek designated gifts from your board members to specifically underwrite planned giving services. Such gifts can be presented as seed money leveraged against future giving, which will endow and expand the future work of the nonprofit.

DONOR-ADVISED FUNDS

One of the fastest-growing planned giving options is a donor-advised fund (DAF), which is a type of charitable giving vehicle set up under the tax umbrella of a charity that acts as a sponsor to many funds. As defined by the National Philanthropic Trust, "A donor-advised fund allows donors to establish and fund an account by making irrevocable, tax-deductible contributions to the charitable sponsor. Donors then recommend grants from those funds to other charitable organizations."[7] Donors receive the tax benefit immediately, including the avoidance of any capital gains taxes in the event that their donated asset appreciates. In turn, they cede ultimate control of the funds to the charity, though typically their recommendation of how to direct those funds bears enormous weight and may be the key "selling point" of the DAF. For example, had it wanted to, the American Canyon Society (first discussed in Chapter 1) could have offered donors the opportunity to name the recipients of the cash stipends ACS provides for scholars to attend environmental conferences.

One of the more attractive features of a DAF is that it obviates the logistical challenges and expenses that donors would incur were they to set up and run a private foundation. From a nonprofit's standpoint, a DAF might be preferable to an outright gift if they sought to establish an endowment to extend in perpetuity.

ESTABLISHING A LEGACY SOCIETY

An absolutely essential task of a robust planned giving program is thanking and recognizing individuals who have remembered your organization in their estate plans. A legacy society is a prestigious "club" open to donors who have made a planned gift to the non-profit upon their deaths. The honor associated with membership in a legacy society encourages others to follow suit and increases the overall number of planned gifts. The names of society members are listed in your annual report and newsletters. For the nonprofit, the society presents yet another highly visible way to create awareness of the planned giving program, while the donors receive a conspicuous acknowledgment of their devotion and generosity to their favorite cause or causes.

Establishing a society is not difficult and can significantly spread interest and awareness of planned giving opportunities among your donors. A simple board resolution establishing your legacy society is enough to get you started. Thereafter, through your gift acceptance policies you can decide which gifts you want to recognize in your society (e.g., larger than $50,000). You'll need to choose a name for your society as well. If you don't want to simply call it The Legacy Society, you can opt to name it after a major donor, a leader in your community, or even a historical figure whose legacy is in line with your program's mission (e.g., The Neil Armstrong Legacy Society). Finally, you must decide how you will acknowledge your legacy society, such as through your newsletter, on your letterhead, or perhaps through an event devoted specifically to it.[8]

No matter how you ultimately shape your planned giving strategy, in order for it to be effective it must regularly identify, cultivate, educate, listen to, meet with, and solicit donors. Donors must be persuaded to think beyond their assets and take a look at how the accumulated value of their estates can help establish a legacy that truly makes a difference during their lives and in perpetuity.

AT THE END OF THE DAY

The concept of planned giving is neither mysterious nor mystical, nor is it just for the elderly. It is for donors of any age who plan ahead and want to make sure your nonprofit maintains financial security. You must actively market the planned giving program to those who are planning oriented, beginning with your own board members. By sharing the details of how planned gifts can work, you create attractive conditions for donors to contribute from their asset portfolios, which, in turn, helps your nonprofit ensure its own financial future.

Active planned giving market programs deliver superior results to passive programs. If you are scrambling to raise cash today, it's because your organization did not pursue planned gifts five or ten years ago. Make this pledge now as one of your ongoing goals: "I pledge that I will do all I can to invite every one of our donors to remember our nonprofit in their will or to make some kind of arrangement benefiting the organization from their estate." An estate gift is arranged during the donor's lifetime but wholly received by the organization upon the donor's death. Obviously, these gifts are made only once, though they can make all the difference to your agency's future.

CONCLUSION

A ZEN MASTER ONCE TOLD me not to bring any books to a meditation retreat I was planning to attend. "Why not?" I asked. "Because books are other people's practice," he said. "They are how others have dealt with their issues and what they have discovered. You are here to make your own discoveries, not read what others have found." With some trepidation, I accepted his counsel and left my books at home.

Naturally, I thought I'd wait until the end of the book to tell you this story. While I hope this book helps you tremendously in moving toward a better set of organizational and fundraising challenges, I also sincerely hope it inspires you to find your own path or, more accurately, the path that will raise more money and take you to the full achievement of your mission.

As fundraisers, we are reminded every day of tough economic times and the ever-increasing competition for funding. But with the proper combination of agility, nimbleness, and self-examination, wedded to a core of the methods that I've outlined throughout the book, you can both achieve your lofty goals and permanently avoid the demoralizing sense of spinning your wheels in vain.

Rather than isolating your organizational development and fundraising programs from each other, you can marry them and—as the Zen master might have put it—create the sound of one world improving.

If you would like to ask Laurence a question or leave your comments about the book, please see www.thenonprofitfundraisingsolution.com. Forms, checklists, and grids that correspond to the book are also to be found there, and you can also sign up there for his free weekly e-newsletter.

Notes

INTRODUCTION

1. Internal Revenue Service, Exempt Organizations Business Master File (2012, October), The Urban Institute, National Center for Charitable Statistics, http://nccs.dataweb.urban.org.
2. Jeanne Bell and Marla Cornelius, *UnderDeveloped: A National Study of Challenges Facing Nonprofit Fundraising* (San Francisco: CompassPoint Nonprofit Services and the Evelyn and Walter Haas, Jr. Fund, 2013), www.compasspoint.org/underdeveloped.
3. Amy S. Blackwood, Katie L. Roeger, and Sarah L. Pettijohn, *The Nonprofit Sector in Brief: Public Charities, Giving, and Volunteering, 2012* (Washington, DC: Urban Institute Press, October 2012).

CHAPTER I: WHY ORGANIZATIONAL CULTURE IS CRITICAL

1. For a comprehensive treatment of the undercapitalization of the nonprofit sector, see Dan Pallotta's work *Uncharitable: How Restraints on Nonprofits Undermine Their Potential* (Lebanon, NH: Tufts University Press, 2009).
2. William Foster and Gail Fine, "How Nonprofits Get Really Big," *Stanford Social Innovation Review,* Spring 2007.

CHAPTER 2: LEADERSHIP FROM THE BELLY OUTWARD

1. Barbara Kellerman, *Followership: How Followers Are Creating and Changing Leaders* (Boston: Harvard Business Press, 2008).
2. Bill Shore, "Shortsighted Charity Donors," *Boston Globe*, December 12, 2004.
3. For a detailed treatment of return on investment and nonprofits, I recommend Tom Ralser's book *ROI for Nonprofits* (New York: John Wiley & Sons, 2007).

CHAPTER 3: TUNING UP THE BOARD FOR EFFECTIVE FUNDRAISING PERFORMANCE

1. George Wright's *Beyond Nominating: A Guide to Gaining and Sustaining Successful Not-for-Profit Boards* (Portland, OR: C3 Publications, 1996) is a resource that helped me to recognize how executives can shape the board to reflect their vision.
2. For a succinct and crisp explication of the legal and ethical responsibilities of every board, also known as the "three duties," go to www.lbnp.org/Websites/lbnp/images/3Ds-Duties-of-care-loyalty-obedience.pdf. The three duties, or the 3Ds, as they are often called, are "the duty of care, the duty of loyalty, and the duty of obedience."
3. Mark Light devotes a book-length analysis to partnerships, cultivated by an aligned executive director and board, in *The Strategic Board: The Step-by-Step Guide to High-Impact Governance* (New York: John Wiley & Sons, 2001).
4. Jim Collins identifies these essential qualities of the great executive in *Good to Great: Why Some Companies Make the Leap and Others Don't* (New York: HarperBusiness, 2001), pp. 39, 216.
5. Peter F. Drucker, *The Five Most Important Questions* (Claremont, CA: The Drucker Institute, 1992; San Francisco: Jossey-Bass, 2008). The 2008 edition was published posthumously.
6. You can find this resource at www.boardsource.org. The Board Self-Assessment (BSA) report makes for a natural agenda for a half-day board retreat, which is, incidentally, an excellent activity to do once or twice a year.
7. *Giving USA: The Annual Report on Philanthropy for the Year 2011* (Chicago: Giving USA Foundation, 2012), www.givingusa.org.
8. James Greenfield's *Fund Raising: Evaluating and Managing the Fund Development Process* (Hoboken, NJ: John Wiley & Sons, 1999) gives national averages of fundraising costs and return on investment; for instance: Direct mail to general lists (nondonors): Cost 115%, ROI 15%. Direct mail to general lists (prior donors): Cost 20%, ROI 80%.

Special events: Cost 50%, ROI 50%. Planned giving: Cost 25%, ROI 75%. Foundations/Corporations: Cost 20%, ROI 80%. Major gifts: Cost 5% to 10%, ROI 90% to 95%. National average, all methods: Cost 20%, ROI 80%.

9. Richard P. Chait, William P. Ryan, and Barbara E. Taylor, *Governance as Leadership: Reframing the Work of Nonprofit Boards* (Hoboken, NJ: John Wiley & Sons, 2004). Chait is a Harvard University Graduate School of Education professor and BoardSource board member. Ryan is a research fellow at the Hauser Center for Nonprofit Organizations at Harvard, and Taylor is a Washington, DC–based consultant.

10. Douglas Stone, Bruce Patton, and Shelia Heen explain how to handle the challenges of these conversations in professional and other settings in *Difficult Conversations: How to Discuss What Matters Most* (New York: Penguin Books, 2010).

11. For a more comprehensive look at how to go from a typical board agenda to a strategic one, I recommend a table designed by my colleague Thomas A. McLaughlin. It is available at www.compasspoint.org/board-cafe/strategic-board-agenda.

CHAPTER 4: HIGHER-LEVEL THINKING FOR GREATER FUNDRAISING PERFORMANCE

1. Dan Pallotta, "We Need to Rethink Fundraising," *Harvard Business Review,* August 9, 2010. The reference to "50 percent to 100 percent" rates means dollar-for-dollar matching (or at least $0.50) for every dollar spent on programs.

2. There have been solid developments in the tools that are available to measure nonprofit performance. *The Nonprofit Outcomes Toolbox* by Robert M. Penna (Hoboken, NJ: John Wiley & Sons, 2011) stands out. This book will help you begin (or advance) your own outcome measurement program.

3. Pallotta, "We Need to Rethink Fundraising," *Harvard Business Review.*

4. William Foster and Gail Fine, "How Nonprofits Get Really Big," *Stanford Social Innovation Review,* Spring 2007, pp. 46–55.

5. Stephen W. Nicholas et al., "Addressing the Childhood Asthma Crisis in Harlem: The Harlem Children's Zone Asthma Initiative," *American Journal of Public Health* 95, no. 2 (February 2005): pp. 245–249.

6. Stephan Lentin, "On Better Communications" (seminar, Richmond, VA, 1988). Dr. Lentin's quote references the work of the famous psychologist Carl Rogers.

7. Jim Collins and Jerry I. Porras, *Built to Last: Successful Habits of Visionary Companies* (New York: HarperBusiness Essentials, 1994).

CHAPTER 5: BUILDING A DONOR CONSTITUENCY WHERE NONE EXISTS

1. National Philanthropic Trust, 2012 Annual Report, www.nptrust.org/philanthropic-resources/charitable-giving-statistics.
2. Two excellent reads about individuals of high net worth are Thomas J. Stanley and William D. Danko, *The Millionaire Next Door* (New York: Simon & Schuster, 1996) and Thomas J. Stanley, *Millionaire Women Next Door* (Kansas City, MO: Andrews McMeel Publishing, 2004).

CHAPTER 7: CHALLENGE GIFT DRIVES AND CORPORATE MATCHING GIFTS

1. About GE Foundation, History, www.ge.com/foundation/about_ge_foundation/history.jsp.
2. Committee Encouraging Corporate Philanthropy (CECP), *Giving in Numbers: 2012 Edition,* www.corporatephilanthropy.org/research/benchmarking-reports/giving-in-numbers.html.

CHAPTER 8: REAPING THE BOUNTY OF YEAR-END GIVING

1. Network for Good and TrueSense Marketing, "The Online Giving Study: A Call to Reinvent Donor Relationships," www.onlinegiving-study.org.
2. Ibid.
3. The Thank-A-Thon concept originated at a soup kitchen I ran for the homeless. We had a large volunteer pool (1,500+) and really needed to nurture and love them. Our volunteers were our pathway to individual donors, and so we asked board members to come to their board meeting an hour early to make some thank-you calls to the other volunteers. Everyone on both ends of the phone call loved it—so much so that we extended the event to an entire day the following year.
4. Dunham+Company, *Direct Mail Growing as a Source for Online Donations,* May 27, 2012.
5. Laurence A. Pagnoni and Sean Jones, "The Evolution of Year-End Appeals: A Conversation with Charlie Whelan," LAPA's Blog, Autumn 2010.
6. "The Online Giving Study" (www.onlinegivingstudy.org).

CHAPTER 9: FUNDRAISING AND RELATIONSHIP BUILDING THROUGH SOCIAL MEDIA

1. Beth Kanter and Allison H. Fine, *The Networked Nonprofit* (San Francisco: Jossey-Bass, 2010).
2. Vinay Bhagat, Dennis McCarthy, and Bryan Snyder, "The Convio Online Marketing Nonprofit Benchmark Index Study" (Austin, TX: Convio, a Blackbaud company, April 2012).
3. "One Thousand Points of 'Like,'" *Economist*, January 7, 2012.

CHAPTER 10: FORMING POWERFUL LEADERSHIP COUNCILS

1. Kim Klein, "Advisory Boards: No Miracle Solution," *Grassroots Fundraising Journal*, October 1982, reprinted in *The Board of Directors*, 3rd ed. (Oakland, CA: Grassroots Fundraising, 2000).

CHAPTER 11: TAKING A NEW APPROACH TO CORPORATE SPONSORSHIPS

1. Committee Encouraging Corporate Philanthropy (CECP), *Giving in Numbers: 2012 Edition*. The 2012 edition on trends in corporate giving is based on data from 214 companies, including 62 of the top 100 companies in the Fortune 500. See www.corporatephilanthropy.org/research/benchmarking-reports/giving-in-numbers.html.

CHAPTER 12: MAJOR FUNDRAISING CAMPAIGNS: THE MORAL EQUIVALENT OF WAR

1. A. C. Marts, *Historical Sketch of the Fund Raising Profession, 1948*; posted to the Marts & Lundy website, martsandlundy.com/sites/default/files/files/ML_Historical_Sketch.pdf.
2. The Urban Institute, http://www.urban.org/nonprofits/index.cfm.
3. Nonprofit Research Collaborative, *Nonprofit Fundraising Study: Covering Charitable Receipts at U.S. Nonprofit Organizations in 2011*. This report, and links to new and earlier reports, can be found at www.NonprofitResearchCollaborative.org or at foundationcenter.org/gainknowledge.
4. W.K. Kellogg has a Template for Strategic Communications Plan that can be downloaded at http://www.wkkf.org/knowledge-center/resources/2006/01/template-for-strategic-communications-plan.aspx.

CHAPTER 13: CREATING OR ADVANCING YOUR PLANNED GIVING PROGRAM

1. Paul Schervish and John Havens, *Millionaires and the Millennium: New Estimates of the Forthcoming Wealth Transfer and the Prospects for a Golden Age of Philanthropy* (Boston College, Social Welfare Research Institute, 1999).
2. Ibid.
3. Center on Philanthropy Panel Study 2007: *Overview of Overall Giving* (Indianapolis, IN: Center on Philanthropy at Indiana University).
4. Giving USA 2012: *The Annual Report on Philanthropy for the Year 2011: Full Report* (Chicago, IL: Giving USA Foundation).
5. 2012 Stelter Donor Insight Report, *What Makes Them Give*, Stelter & Co., www.stelter.com/research-whitepapers/WhatMakesThemGive-2012Research.pdf.
6. Emily Krauser, *Bequest Donors: Demographics and Motivations of Potential and Actual Donors,* Campbell & Company and the Center on Philanthropy at Indiana University, March 2007.
7. National Philanthropic Trust, *2012 Donor-Advised Fund Report,* www.nptrust.org/daf-report/.
8. *A Guide to Building a Legacy Society* (Grand Haven, MI: Council of Michigan Foundations, 1995).

INDEX